William Shakespeare's

King Henry VIII
In Plain and Simple English

■BŌŌKCAPS

A SwipeSpeare™ Book
www.SwipeSpeare.com

Table of Contents:

About This Series

The "SwipeSpeare™" series started as a way of telling Shakespeare for the modern reader—being careful to preserve the themes and integrity of the original. Visit our website SwipeSpeare.com to see other books in the series, as well as the interactive, and swipe-able, app!

The series is expanding every month. Visit BookCaps.com to see non-Shakespeare books in this series, and while you are there join the Facebook page, so you are first to know when a new book comes out.

Characters

Queen Katharine

Sir Nicholas Vaux

Sir Henry Guildford

Griffith

King Henry VIII of England

Patience

Sir William Sands

Cardinal Wolsey

Sir Thomas Lovell

Stephen Gardiner

Thomas Cromwell

Brandon

Doctor Butts

Cardinal Campeius

Anne Boleyn

Lord Abergavenny

Sir Anthony Denny

Lord Capuchius

Marquess Dorset

Marquis Dorset

Princess Elizabeth

Lord Chancellor

Lord Chamberlain

Cranmer

Prologue

I come no more to make you laugh: things now,
That bear a weighty and a serious brow,
Sad, high, and working, full of state and woe,
Such noble scenes as draw the eye to flow,
We now present. Those that can pity, here
May, if they think it well, let fall a tear;
The subject will deserve it. Such as give
Their money out of hope they may believe,
May here find truth too. Those that come to see
Only a show or two, and so agree
The play may pass, if they be still and willing,
I'll undertake may see away their shilling
Richly in two short hours. Only they
That come to hear a merry bawdy play,
A noise of targets, or to see a fellow
In a long motley coat guarded with yellow,
Will be deceived; for, gentle hearers, know,
To rank our chosen truth with such a show
As fool and fight is, beside forfeiting
Our own brains, and the opinion that we bring,
To make that only true we now intend,
Will leave us never an understanding friend.
Therefore, for goodness' sake, and as you are known
The first and happiest hearers of the town,
Be sad, as we would make ye: think ye see
The very persons of our noble story
As they were living; think you see them great,
And follow'd with the general throng and sweat
Of thousand friends; then in a moment, see
How soon this mightiness meets misery:
And, if you can be merry then, I'll say
A man may weep upon his wedding-day.

*I'm no longer here to make you laugh; now
we're dealing with heavy serious matters,
serious, lofty and moving, full of dignity and sorrow;
we will now present noble scenes which will
provoke your tears. Those who can pity may
now (if they think it right) shed a tear,
the subject will deserve it. Those who put
their money down to see something believable*

may find truth here too. Those who just come
for the spectacle, that's what makes them
say a play is good, if they keep still with an open mind,
I promise that they will get their shillingsworth
in two quickly passing hours. Only the ones
who have come to hear a jolly smutty play,
hear clashing shields, or to see a fellow
in a yellow trimmed clown costume,
will be disappointed: for, gentle listeners,
to show the truth we want through
comedy and fight scenes, besides spoiling
the work of our brains and
our intention to show nothing but the truth,
would make our audience abandon us.
Therefore, for goodness sake, as you are renowned
as the most important and tolerant audience in the town,
 be serious, as we want you to be. Imagine you see
the characters of our noble story
as if they were alive: imagine you see them in their greatness,
followed by great crowds, the toil
of a thousand friends; then, in the blink of an eye, see
how quickly greatness can become miserable:
and if you can be jolly then, I will say
a man can weep on his wedding day.

Act I

SCENE I. London. An ante-chamber in the palace.

Enter NORFOLK at one door; at the other, BUCKINGHAM and ABERGAVENNY

BUCKINGHAM
Good morrow, and well met. How have ye done
Since last we saw in France?

*Good day, and welcome. How have you been
since we last met in France?*

NORFOLK
I thank your grace,
Healthful; and ever since a fresh admirer
Of what I saw there.

*Very well, thank you
your Grace; and I have not lost my admiration
for what I saw there.*

BUCKINGHAM
An untimely ague
Stay'd me a prisoner in my chamber when
Those suns of glory, those two lights of men,
Met in the vale of Andren.

*An inconvenient fever
kept me a prisoner in my room when
those two glorious suns, those examples to mankind,
met in the Vale of Andren.*

NORFOLK
'Twixt Guynes and Arde:
I was then present, saw them salute on horseback;
Beheld them, when they lighted, how they clung
In their embracement, as they grew together;
Which had they, what four throned ones could have weigh'd
Such a compounded one?

*Between Guynes and Arde:
I was there at the time, and saw them greet each other on horseback;
I saw how when they dismounted they hugged*

each other, as if they were a single being;
if they were, what four Kings could have matched
one such combination?

BUCKINGHAM
All the whole time
I was my chamber's prisoner.

I was confined to my room
the whole time.

NORFOLK
Then you lost
The view of earthly glory: men might say,
Till this time pomp was single, but now married
To one above itself. Each following day
Became the next day's master, till the last
Made former wonders its. To-day the French,
All clinquant, all in gold, like heathen gods,
Shone down the English; and, to-morrow, they
Made Britain India: every man that stood
Show'd like a mine. Their dwarfish pages were
As cherubins, all guilt: the madams too,
Not used to toil, did almost sweat to bear
The pride upon them, that their very labour
Was to them as a painting: now this masque
Was cried incomparable; and the ensuing night
Made it a fool and beggar. The two kings,
Equal in lustre, were now best, now worst,
As presence did present them; him in eye,
Still him in praise: and, being present both
'Twas said they saw but one; and no discerner
Durst wag his tongue in censure. When these suns--
For so they phrase 'em--by their heralds challenged
The noble spirits to arms, they did perform
Beyond thought's compass; that former fabulous story,
Being now seen possible enough, got credit,
That Bevis was believed.

Then you missed
a sight of glory on earth: men might say
that grandeur was single up to now, before it married
one even greater. Every successive day
showed greater pageantry than the rest, until the last one
combined everything that had gone before. One day the French,
all glittering with gold, outshone the English

like heathen gods; and the next day
the English would display the riches of India; every man
look like a goldmine. Their little pages looked
like cherubim, all gilded: the ladies too,
unused to labour, were almost sweating to carry
the riches upon them, so that their work
brought colour to their cheeks. So this show
would be called unbeatable; and the next night
it looks like the work of a foolish beggar. The two kings,
equal in glory, were now the best, then the worst,
depending whose turn it was: with them
both there to be seen they were praised equally,
men said they could only see one king, and no
observer dared to voice any criticism. When these suns
(for that's what they call them) were challenged by their heralds
to joust with each other, they did it
better than one could imagine, they were so good
that it was now seen how former feats of arms,
previously thought legendary, could have been true.

BUCKINGHAM
O, you go far.

Oh, you're being very effusive.

NORFOLK
As I belong to worship and affect
In honour honesty, the tract of every thing
Would by a good discourser lose some life,
Which action's self was tongue to. All was royal;
To the disposing of it nought rebell'd.
Order gave each thing view; the office did
Distinctly his full function.

As God is my witness and as I
worship honesty, I tell you that
there are not words good enough to describe
the things that went on. Everything was royal;
nothing was spared in showing it,
everything was in its place: the officials did
their tasks perfectly.

BUCKINGHAM
Who did guide,
I mean, who set the body and the limbs
Of this great sport together, as you guess?

Who ran the show,
I mean, who ordered all the elements
of this great business, do you think?

NORFOLK
One, certes, that promises no element
In such a business.

One who you most certainly wouldn't imagine
would have the skills for such a business.

BUCKINGHAM
I pray you, who, my lord?

Tell me, who, my lord?

NORFOLK
All this was order'd by the good discretion
Of the right reverend Cardinal of York.

Everything was done under the orders
of the right reverend Cardinal of York.

BUCKINGHAM
The devil speed him! no man's pie is freed
From his ambitious finger. What had he
To do in these fierce vanities? I wonder
That such a keech can with his very bulk
Take up the rays o' the beneficial sun
And keep it from the earth.

A curse on him! There is no pie in which
he doesn't have his ambitious fingers. What was his
business with these extravagances? I'm amazed
that such a lump is able to occupy
the King so much and keep him from
the general public.

NORFOLK
Surely, sir,
There's in him stuff that puts him to these ends;
For, being not propp'd by ancestry, whose grace
Chalks successors their way, nor call'd upon
For high feats done to the crown; neither allied

For eminent assistants; but, spider-like,
Out of his self-drawing web, he gives us note,
The force of his own merit makes his way
A gift that heaven gives for him, which buys
A place next to the king.

Surely, Sir,
there's a reason that he's like this;
he is not supported by great ancestry,
which gives descendants examples to follow, nor is he
valued for great acts done on behalf of the Crown;
nor is he related to great ministers; but, like a spider,
he gets his position from his own self-made web,
he makes his way by his own merits,
the gift that heaven has given him, which buys him
a place next to the King.

ABERGAVENNY
I cannot tell
What heaven hath given him,--let some graver eye
Pierce into that; but I can see his pride
Peep through each part of him: whence has he that?
If not from hell the devil is a niggard,
Or has given all before, and he begins
A new hell in himself.

I don't know
what heaven has given him—let someone more
experienced look into that; but I can see his pride
shining out of every part of him: where has he got that from?
If not from hell then the devil is miserly,
or has given away all his pride, and Wolsey begins
a new hell himself.

BUCKINGHAM
Why the devil,
Upon this French going out, took he upon him,
Without the privity o' the king, to appoint
Who should attend on him? He makes up the file
Of all the gentry; for the most part such
To whom as great a charge as little honour
He meant to lay upon: and his own letter,
The honourable board of council out,
Must fetch him in the papers.

Why the devil did he,

at the start of this French expedition, assume,
without the King's knowledge, the responsibility of choosing
who should go with him? He chose which
gentlemen should go; mostly those on whom
he intended to impose a great tax without
giving them any honour: they were ordered to come
by his own letter, he didn't bother consulting with
the honourable board of Council.

ABERGAVENNY
I do know
Kinsmen of mine, three at the least, that have
By this so sickened their estates, that never
They shall abound as formerly.

I know
at least three relatives of mine who have
had to spend so much on this business that
their estates will never recover.

BUCKINGHAM
O, many
Have broke their backs with laying manors on 'em
For this great journey. What did this vanity
But minister communication of
A most poor issue?

O, many
have acquired a great deal of property
through this expedition. What use was this extravagance
apart from stealing away the
inheritance of children?

NORFOLK
Grievingly I think,
The peace between the French and us not values
The cost that did conclude it.

I'm sorry to say,
the peace concluded between the French and us is not worth
the price we paid for it.

BUCKINGHAM
Every man,
After the hideous storm that follow'd, was
A thing inspired; and, not consulting, broke

Into a general prophecy; That this tempest,
Dashing the garment of this peace, aboded
The sudden breach on't.

After the hideous storm that followed the
signing of the peace every man became inspired,
and spontaneously everyone began to prophesy
that the storm, raging against the peace, showed
that it would be broken.

NORFOLK
Which is budded out;
For France hath flaw'd the league, and hath attach'd
Our merchants' goods at Bourdeaux.

And this has come to fruition;
for France has broken the deal, and has seized
our merchants' goods at Bordeaux.

ABERGAVENNY
Is it therefore
The ambassador is silenced?

Does that mean
the ambassador has been prevented from speaking?

NORFOLK
Marry, is't.

It certainly does.

ABERGAVENNY
A proper title of a peace; and purchased
At a superfluous rate!

A fine thing to call peace; and bought
at such a high price!

BUCKINGHAM
Why, all this business
Our reverend cardinal carried.

Why, all this business
was down to our reverend cardinal.

NORFOLK

Like it your grace,
The state takes notice of the private difference
Betwixt you and the cardinal. I advise you--
And take it from a heart that wishes towards you
Honour and plenteous safety--that you read
The cardinal's malice and his potency
Together; to consider further that
What his high hatred would effect wants not
A minister in his power. You know his nature,
That he's revengeful, and I know his sword
Hath a sharp edge: it's long and, 't may be said,
It reaches far, and where 'twill not extend,
Thither he darts it. Bosom up my counsel,
You'll find it wholesome. Lo, where comes that rock
That I advise your shunning.

If I may say so your Grace,
everyone has noticed the private disagreement
between you and the Cardinal. I advise you–
and accept it from a heart who wishes you
honour and all safety–that you consider
the cardinal's malice and his power
together; and think further that
he's not lacking ministers to carry out
his hatred. You know what he's like,
that he holds a grudge,
and I know his sword
is sharp: it's long, and one may say
it can reach far places, and where it won't reach,
he throws it. Remember my advice,
you will find it beneficial. Look, here comes the rock
that I advise you to steer clear of.

Enter CARDINAL WOLSEY, the purse borne before him, certain of the Guard, and two
Secretaries with papers. CARDINAL WOLSEY in his passage fixeth his eye on BUCKINGHAM,
and BUCKINGHAM on him, both full of disdain

CARDINAL WOLSEY
The Duke of Buckingham's surveyor, ha?
Where's his examination?

The Duke of Buckingham's surveyor, ha?
Where is his testimony?

First Secretary
Here, so please you.

Here, if you please.

CARDINAL WOLSEY
Is he in person ready?

Is he ready in person?

First Secretary
Ay, please your grace.

Yes, if your Grace pleases.

CARDINAL WOLSEY
Well, we shall then know more; and Buckingham
Shall lessen this big look.

Well then, we shall no more; and Buckingham
shall stop looking so haughty.

Exeunt CARDINAL WOLSEY and his Train

BUCKINGHAM
This butcher's cur is venom-mouth'd, and I
Have not the power to muzzle him; therefore best
Not wake him in his slumber. A beggar's book
Outworths a noble's blood.

This butcher's dog has a poisonous mouth, and I
do not have the power to muzzle him; so it's best
not to wake him up. A beggar's learning
is worth more than any noble descent.

NORFOLK
What, are you chafed?
Ask God for temperance; that's the appliance only
Which your disease requires.

What, are you angry?
Ask God for self-control; that's the only medicine
your disease requires.

BUCKINGHAM
I read in's looks
Matter against me; and his eye reviled
Me, as his abject object: at this instant

He bores me with some trick: he's gone to the king;
I'll follow and outstare him.

I can see in his eyes
that he has plans against me; he looked at me
contemptuously; right now
he is cheating me with some trick; he has gone to the King:
I'll follow him and outstare him.

NORFOLK
Stay, my lord,
And let your reason with your choler question
What 'tis you go about: to climb steep hills
Requires slow pace at first: anger is like
A full-hot horse, who being allow'd his way,
Self-mettle tires him. Not a man in England
Can advise me like you: be to yourself
As you would to your friend.

Wait, my lord,
and think dispassionately about
what you are doing: to climb steep hills
you need to go slowly at first: anger is like
a passionate horse, if you allow it its head
it will soon tire itself out. There's not a man in England
who can advise me like you: be a good friend
to yourself.

BUCKINGHAM
I'll to the king;
And from a mouth of honour quite cry down
This Ipswich fellow's insolence; or proclaim
There's difference in no persons.

I'll go to the King;
and with the mouth of honour I will shout down
the insolence of this Ipswich fellow; otherwise I'll say
that all men are equal.

NORFOLK
Be advised;
Heat not a furnace for your foe so hot
That it do singe yourself: we may outrun,
By violent swiftness, that which we run at,
And lose by over-running. Know you not,
The fire that mounts the liquor til run o'er,

In seeming to augment it wastes it? Be advised:
I say again, there is no English soul
More stronger to direct you than yourself,
If with the sap of reason you would quench,
Or but allay, the fire of passion.

Be sensible;
don't prepare a furnace for your enemy that's so hot
that you burn yourself: when we charge at something
we can outrun it with violent swiftness, and miss it
by overrunning it. Don't you know that
the fire that heats the liquor until it boils over
seems to make it greater but in fact wastes it? Be sensible:
I tell you again there is no man in England
who can give you better advice than yourself,
if you will put out the fire of passion, or at least
damp it down, with the water of reason.

BUCKINGHAM
Sir,
I am thankful to you; and I'll go along
By your prescription: but this top-proud fellow,
Whom from the flow of gall I name not but
From sincere motions, by intelligence,
And proofs as clear as founts in July when
We see each grain of gravel, I do know
To be corrupt and treasonous.

Sir,
I am grateful to you; and I will follow
your advice: but I know that this arrogant fellow,
whom I'm not accusing through anger but
from sincere motives, through intelligence,
and proof as clear as springs in July when
we can see each grain of gravel,
is corrupt and treasonous.

NORFOLK
Say not 'treasonous.'

Do not say 'treasonous.'

BUCKINGHAM
To the king I'll say't; and make my vouch as strong
As shore of rock. Attend. This holy fox,
Or wolf, or both,--for he is equal ravenous

As he is subtle, and as prone to mischief
As able to perform't; his mind and place
Infecting one another, yea, reciprocally--
Only to show his pomp as well in France
As here at home, suggests the king our master
To this last costly treaty, the interview,
That swallow'd so much treasure, and like a glass
Did break i' the rinsing.

I shall say to the King; and I shall give proof as strong
as rocky cliffs. Listen. This holy fox,
or wolf, or both,–for he is as ravenous
as he is cunning, and as eager for mischief
as he is able to perform it; his thoughts and actions
infect each other, to and fro–
just to show his eminence in France
as much as here at home, has suggested to our master the King
that we should make this recent costly treaty, the meeting
for which cost so much money, and which shattered like glass
the first time it was put to the test.

NORFOLK
Faith, and so it did.

It did indeed.

BUCKINGHAM
Pray, give me favour, sir. This cunning cardinal
The articles o' the combination drew
As himself pleased; and they were ratified
As he cried 'Thus let be': to as much end
As give a crutch to the dead: but our count-cardinal
Has done this, and 'tis well; for worthy Wolsey,
Who cannot err, he did it. Now this follows,--
Which, as I take it, is a kind of puppy
To the old dam, treason,--Charles the emperor,
Under pretence to see the queen his aunt--
For 'twas indeed his colour, but he came
To whisper Wolsey,--here makes visitation:
His fears were, that the interview betwixt
England and France might, through their amity,
Breed him some prejudice; for from this league
Peep'd harms that menaced him: he privily
Deals with our cardinal; and, as I trow,--
Which I do well; for I am sure the emperor
Paid ere he promised; whereby his suit was granted

Ere it was ask'd; but when the way was made,
And paved with gold, the emperor thus desired,
That he would please to alter the king's course,
And break the foresaid peace. Let the king know,
As soon he shall by me, that thus the cardinal
Does buy and sell his honour as he pleases,
And for his own advantage.

Please listen to me, sir: this cunning cardinal
drew up the terms of the treaty
just as he wished; and they were agreed
on his say-so, and they are as useful
as a crutch for the dead. But our royal cardinal
has done this, and it's good; for worthy Wolsey,
who can do no wrong, has done it. Now what's happening
(which I assume is the offspring of treason) is that the
Emperor Charles, under pretence of coming to see his aunt the Queen
(that's what he said, but he really came
to confer with Wolsey) is visiting here;
he was worried that the meeting between
England and France might, through their friendship,
do him some harm, for he saw a threat to him
in their agreement: he secretly
deals with our cardinal, and I believe
(which I have good cause for, for I'm sure the Emperor
paid before he asked, so his wishes were granted
at once) that once the path had been
laid down with money the Emperor asked
him to change the King's course
and break the previously agreed peace. The King must know
(and I shall soon tell him) that this is how the cardinal
buys and sells his honour as he pleases,
for his own advantage.

NORFOLK
I am sorry
To hear this of him; and could wish he were
Something mistaken in't.

I'm sorry
to hear this from you; and I hope
you are somewhat mistaken.

BUCKINGHAM
No, not a syllable:
I do pronounce him in that very shape

He shall appear in proof.

No, every word is true:
I have described exactly what
my proof shall show.

Enter BRANDON, a Sergeant-at-arms before him, and two or three of the Guard

BRANDON
Your office, sergeant; execute it.

Do your duty, sergeant.

Sergeant
Sir,
My lord the Duke of Buckingham, and Earl
Of Hereford, Stafford, and Northampton, I
Arrest thee of high treason, in the name
Of our most sovereign king.

Sir,
my lord the Duke of Buckingham, Earl
of Hereford, Stafford and Northampton, I
arrest you for high treason, in the name
of our Majestic King.

BUCKINGHAM
Lo, you, my lord,
The net has fall'n upon me! I shall perish
Under device and practise.

You see my lord,
the net has fallen over me! I shall die
through tricks and intrigue.

BRANDON
I am sorry
To see you ta'en from liberty, to look on
The business present: 'tis his highness' pleasure
You shall to the Tower.

I am sorry
to see you lose your freedom, to be witness to
this business: his Highness desires that you
be sent to the Tower.

BUCKINGHAM
It will help me nothing
To plead mine innocence; for that dye is on me
Which makes my whitest part black. The will of heaven
Be done in this and all things! I obey.
O my Lord Abergavenny, fare you well!

There won't be any use
in pleading my innocence; the stain has been cast on me
which makes my most innocent parts seem guilty. May the will of heaven
be done in this and in everything! I shall obey.
Oh my Lord Abergavenny, farewell!

BRANDON
Nay, he must bear you company. The king
To ABERGAVENNY
Is pleased you shall to the Tower, till you know
How he determines further.

No, he's coming with you. The King
wants you to go to the Tower, to await
his further orders.

ABERGAVENNY
As the duke said,
The will of heaven be done, and the king's pleasure
By me obey'd!

As the Duke said,
May the will of heaven be done, and may I obey
the king's orders!

BRANDON
Here is a warrant from
The king to attach Lord Montacute; and the bodies
Of the duke's confessor, John de la Car,
One Gilbert Peck, his chancellor--

Here is a warrant from
the King to arrest Lord Montacute; also
the Duke's confessor, John de la Car,
his Chancellor, Gilbert Peck–

BUCKINGHAM
So, so;
These are the limbs o' the plot: no more, I hope.

Alright, alright;
the plot is obvious: no more, I hope.

BRANDON
A monk o' the Chartreux.

A Carthusian monk.

BUCKINGHAM
O, Nicholas Hopkins?

Oh, Nicholas Hopkins?

BRANDON
He.

Him.

BUCKINGHAM
My surveyor is false; the o'er-great cardinal
Hath show'd him gold; my life is spann'd already:
I am the shadow of poor Buckingham,
Whose figure even this instant cloud puts on,
By darkening my clear sun. My lord, farewell.

My surveyor is a traitor; the too powerful cardinal
has bribed him; my life is already lost:
I am the ghost of poor Buckingham,
who now walks in the shadows,
his sun is darkened. My lord, farewell.
Exeunt

SCENE II. The same. The council-chamber.

Cornets. Enter KING HENRY VIII, leaning on CARDINAL WOLSEY's shoulder, the Nobles, and LOVELL; CARDINAL WOLSEY places himself under KING HENRY VIII's feet on his right side

KING HENRY VIII
My life itself, and the best heart of it,
Thanks you for this great care: I stood i' the level
Of a full-charged confederacy, and give thanks
To you that choked it. Let be call'd before us
That gentleman of Buckingham's; in person
I'll hear him his confessions justify;
And point by point the treasons of his master
He shall again relate.

My life itself, and the very best part of it,
thanks you for your excellent work: I was threatened
by a full-blown conspiracy, and I thank
you who cut it off. Someone bring before us
that gentleman of Buckingham's; I'll hear him
explain his evidence in person;
he shall retell the treason of his master
point by point.

A noise within, crying 'Room for the Queen!' Enter QUEEN KATHARINE, ushered by NORFOLK, and SUFFOLK: she kneels. KING HENRY VIII riseth from his state, takes her up, kisses and placeth her by him

QUEEN KATHARINE
Nay, we must longer kneel: I am a suitor.

No, I must remain on my knees: I have come to beg.

KING HENRY VIII
Arise, and take place by us: half your suit
Never name to us; you have half our power:
The other moiety, ere you ask, is given;
Repeat your will and take it.

Get up, and take your place by me: don't mention
half of what you want; you have half my power:

the other share is given before you ask;
say what you want and you shall have it.

QUEEN KATHARINE
Thank your majesty.
That you would love yourself, and in that love
Not unconsider'd leave your honour, nor
The dignity of your office, is the point
Of my petition.

I thank your Majesty.
What I want is that you should
love yourself, and in your love
you should not forget your honour,
nor the dignity of your office.

KING HENRY VIII
Lady mine, proceed.

My lady, go on.

QUEEN KATHARINE
I am solicited, not by a few,
And those of true condition, that your subjects
Are in great grievance: there have been commissions
Sent down among 'em, which hath flaw'd the heart
Of all their loyalties: wherein, although,
My good lord cardinal, they vent reproaches
Most bitterly on you, as putter on
Of these exactions, yet the king our master--
Whose honour heaven shield from soil!--even he
escapes not
Language unmannerly, yea, such which breaks
The sides of loyalty, and almost appears
In loud rebellion.

I have been advised by many,
of noble position, that your subjects
are very unhappy: orders have been
distributed which have almost killed
their loyalty: although they have
saved their most bitter reproaches
for you, my good lord cardinal, as the
creator of these burdens, but the King our master–
may heaven prevent his honour being stained!–
even he does not escape from

rude language, which escapes from loyal people
and seems to be almost a rebellion.

NORFOLK
Not almost appears,
It doth appear; for, upon these taxations,
The clothiers all, not able to maintain
The many to them longing, have put off
The spinsters, carders, fullers, weavers, who,
Unfit for other life, compell'd by hunger
And lack of other means, in desperate manner
Daring the event to the teeth, are all in uproar,
And danger serves among them.

Not just almost,
it actually is; for, due to these taxes,
the tailors, unable to support
those who rely on them, have laid off
the spinners, carders, dyers and weavers who,
unable to find other work, driven by hunger
and lack of income, have been challenging
the matter with open defiance, they are in uproar,
and the situation is very dangerous.

KING HENRY VIII
Taxation!
Wherein? and what taxation? My lord cardinal,
You that are blamed for it alike with us,
Know you of this taxation?

Taxation!
How? And what taxation? My lord cardinal,
who is blamed for it alongside me,
do you know about this taxation?

CARDINAL WOLSEY
Please you, sir,
I know but of a single part, in aught
Pertains to the state; and front but in that file
Where others tell steps with me.

If you please, sir,
I only know my own business
in matters of state, and I'm just the most prominent
of all those who are doing the same.

QUEEN KATHARINE
No, my lord,
You know no more than others; but you frame
Things that are known alike; which are not wholesome
To those which would not know them, and yet must
Perforce be their acquaintance. These exactions,
Whereof my sovereign would have note, they are
Most pestilent to the bearing; and, to bear 'em,
The back is sacrifice to the load. They say
They are devised by you; or else you suffer
Too hard an exclamation.

No, my lord,
you know no more than others; but you
make the plans that everyone knows;
they are not agreeable to those they do not benefit,
but everyone has to agree to them. These taxes,
which my sovereign wants to hear of, are
a terrible burden, and to carry them
breaks the back of those who suffer them. They say
you invented them; otherwise you are
unfairly cursed.

KING HENRY VIII
Still exaction!
The nature of it? in what kind, let's know,
Is this exaction?

Still talking about taxes!
What taxes? I want to know
what type of taxes these are.

QUEEN KATHARINE
I am much too venturous
In tempting of your patience; but am bolden'd
Under your promised pardon. The subjects' grief
Comes through commissions, which compel from each
The sixth part of his substance, to be levied
Without delay; and the pretence for this
Is named, your wars in France: this makes bold mouths:
Tongues spit their duties out, and cold hearts freeze
Allegiance in them; their curses now
Live where their prayers did: and it's come to pass,
This tractable obedience is a slave
To each incensed will. I would your highness
Would give it quick consideration, for

There is no primer business.

I am far too forward
in testing your patience; but your promised forgiveness
emboldens me. The subjects' grievance
is with the writs, which demand from everyone
a sixth of his fortune, to be paid
at once; the excuse for this is given
as paying for your wars in France; this makes men speak boldly:
tongues reject their duties, and cold hearts
shun their loyalty; where once they prayed for you
 they now curse you; and their obedience
has been replaced by their anger. I hope your highness
will give this urgent consideration; for
there's nothing needs dealing with more urgently.

KING HENRY VIII
By my life,
This is against our pleasure.

I swear,
I didn't want this.

CARDINAL WOLSEY
And for me,
I have no further gone in this than by
A single voice; and that not pass'd me but
By learned approbation of the judges. If I am
Traduced by ignorant tongues, which neither know
My faculties nor person, yet will be
The chronicles of my doing, let me say
'Tis but the fate of place, and the rough brake
That virtue must go through. We must not stint
Our necessary actions, in the fear
To cope malicious censurers; which ever,
As ravenous fishes, do a vessel follow
That is new-trimm'd, but benefit no further
Than vainly longing. What we oft do best,
By sick interpreters, once weak ones, is
Not ours, or not allow'd; what worst, as oft,
Hitting a grosser quality, is cried up
For our best act. If we shall stand still,
In fear our motion will be mock'd or carp'd at,
We should take root here where we sit, or sit
State-statues only.

As for me,
I have done no more in this than was ordered
by a unanimous vote; and that was not passed by me but
by the learned deliberations of the judges: if I am
defamed by ignorant men, who do not know
my abilities or my character, but want to
judge my actions, let me say
that is just the burden of office, and the rough road
that virtue must travel: we must not allow
our necessary actions to be prescribed
to please malicious critics, who are like sharks
who follow a sound seaworthy ship, who get nothing
beyond their vain desires. What we do best
is often not acknowledged or attributed to
others by envious or faithless interpreters;
our worst, finding favour with low people,
is praised as our best. If we stand still,
fearing that if we move we will be mocked or criticised,
we would take root here, where we sit;
we would just be figureheads.

KING HENRY VIII
Things done well,
And with a care, exempt themselves from fear;
Things done without example, in their issue
Are to be fear'd. Have you a precedent
Of this commission? I believe, not any.
We must not rend our subjects from our laws,
And stick them in our will. Sixth part of each?
A trembling contribution! Why, we take
From every tree lop, bark, and part o' the timber;
And, though we leave it with a root, thus hack'd,
The air will drink the sap. To every county
Where this is question'd send our letters, with
Free pardon to each man that has denied
The force of this commission: pray, look to't;
I put it to your care.

Things which are done well
and carefully are not to be worried about;
we have to be concerned about things done
without precedent. Do you have a precedent
for these writs? I don't believe you have.
We must not treat our subjects according to our will,
instead of by the law. A sixth of everyone's fortune?
A fearful imposition! Why, if we took

the twigs, bark and part of the timber from every tree,
even if we left its roots, chopped like that
the air would dry up the sap. Send letters to
every county that has resisted this tax
and say that I give a free pardon to every man
who has refused to pay it: please take care of it,
I'm leaving it to you.

CARDINAL WOLSEY
[To the Secretary]
A word with you.
Let there be letters writ to every shire,
Of the king's grace and pardon. The grieved commons
Hardly conceive of me; let it be noised
That through our intercession this revokement
And pardon comes: I shall anon advise you
Further in the proceeding.

Listen to me.
Write letters to every county,
telling them of the King's grace and pardon. The angry people
hardly know anything about me; put it about
that it was my intervention which caused this repeal
and pardon: I'll tell you soon what else
I want you to do.

Exit Secretary
Enter Surveyor

QUEEN KATHARINE
I am sorry that the Duke of Buckingham
Is run in your displeasure.

I am sorry that the Duke of Buckingham
has incurred your displeasure.

KING HENRY VIII
It grieves many:
The gentleman is learn'd, and a most rare speaker;
To nature none more bound; his training such,
That he may furnish and instruct great teachers,
And never seek for aid out of himself. Yet see,
When these so noble benefits shall prove
Not well disposed, the mind growing once corrupt,
They turn to vicious forms, ten times more ugly
Than ever they were fair. This man so complete,

Who was enroll'd 'mongst wonders, and when we,
Almost with ravish'd listening, could not find
His hour of speech a minute; he, my lady,
Hath into monstrous habits put the graces
That once were his, and is become as black
As if besmear'd in hell. Sit by us; you shall hear--
This was his gentleman in trust--of him
Things to strike honour sad. Bid him recount
The fore-recited practises; whereof
We cannot feel too little, hear too much.

Many are sorry for it:
the gentleman is learned, and a great speaker,
nobody is more naturally gifted; so much so
that he could educate great teachers,
and never need any help apart from himself: but look,
when these great virtues are not used
for good, wants the mind becomes corrupt,
they turn to evil purposes, ten times more ugly
than their original beauty. This man who was so complete,
who was thought of as a wonder–when I
listen to him, entranced, an hour of him speaking
seemed to be hardly a minute–he, my lady,
has used the gifts he once had
for monstrous purposes, and has become as evil
as if he was touched by hell. Sit next to me, you shall hear
from this gentleman who was his confidential servant things
which will make honour sad. Tell him to repeat
the matters he's spoken of, of which
we cannot hear enough, or feel too little.

CARDINAL WOLSEY
Stand forth, and with bold spirit relate what you,
Most like a careful subject, have collected
Out of the Duke of Buckingham.

Step forward, and fearlessly tell us what you
have, like a good subject, learned about
the Duke of Buckingham.

KING HENRY VIII
Speak freely.

Speak freely.

Surveyor

First, it was usual with him, every day
It would infect his speech, that if the king
Should without issue die, he'll carry it so
To make the sceptre his: these very words
I've heard him utter to his son-in-law,
Lord Abergavenny; to whom by oath he menaced
Revenge upon the cardinal.

Firstly, it was a usual thing with him,
he would say it every day, that if the King
died without an heir, he would seize
the kingship for himself: I've heard him say
these very words to his son-in-law,
Lord Abergavenny; he swore to him
that he would have revenge on the cardinal.

CARDINAL WOLSEY
Please your highness, note
This dangerous conception in this point.
Not friended by his wish, to your high person
His will is most malignant, and it stretches
Beyond you, to your friends.

Would your Highness please note
the dangerous thoughts expressed here.
Unsuccessful in his wishes against your Highness
his desires are most malignant, and they stretch
beyond you to attack your friends.

QUEEN KATHARINE
My learn'd lord cardinal,
Deliver all with charity.

My learned lord cardinal,
try to speak charitably.

KING HENRY VIII
Speak on:
How grounded he his title to the crown,
Upon our fail? to this point hast thou heard him
At any time speak aught?

Carry on:
how did he justify his claim to the throne,
if I had no heirs? Have you heard him say anything
about this?

Surveyor
He was brought to this
By a vain prophecy of Nicholas Hopkins.

He was encouraged to think of this
by an empty prophecy of Nicholas Hopkins.

KING HENRY VIII
What was that Hopkins?

Who is this Hopkins?

Surveyor
Sir, a Chartreux friar,
His confessor, who fed him every minute
With words of sovereignty.

Sir, a Carthusian friar,
his confessor, who at every minute encouraged him
to think he had a claim to the throne.

KING HENRY VIII
How know'st thou this?

How do you know this?

Surveyor
Not long before your highness sped to France,
The duke being at the Rose, within the parish
Saint Lawrence Poultney, did of me demand
What was the speech among the Londoners
Concerning the French journey: I replied,
Men fear'd the French would prove perfidious,
To the king's danger. Presently the duke
Said, 'twas the fear, indeed; and that he doubted
'Twould prove the verity of certain words
Spoke by a holy monk; 'that oft,' says he,
'Hath sent to me, wishing me to permit
John de la Car, my chaplain, a choice hour
To hear from him a matter of some moment:
Whom after under the confession's seal
He solemnly had sworn, that what he spoke
My chaplain to no creature living, but
To me, should utter, with demure confidence
This pausingly ensued: neither the king nor's heirs,

Tell you the duke, shall prosper: bid him strive
To gain the love o' the commonalty: the duke
Shall govern England.'

Not long before your Highness went to France,
the Duke was at the Rose, in the parish
of St Laurence Poultney, and he asked me
what Londoners were saying about your French expedition: I replied
that people were afraid the French would be untrustworthy,
to the peril of the King. At once the Duke said
that was indeed a worry; and that he feared
it would prove the truth of certain words
spoken by a holy monk; he had often, he said,
sent him messages, asking him to permit
John de la Car, his chaplain, to find the time
when he could tell him some important matter:
after he had solemnly sworn under the seal
of confession that he would not tell any living creature
but the Duke what he said he haltingly but with
solemn assurance said this, that he should tell the Duke
that neither the king nor his heirs will prosper; that he should
strive to win over the love of the people; the Duke
will govern England.

QUEEN KATHARINE
If I know you well,
You were the duke's surveyor, and lost your office
On the complaint o' the tenants: take good heed
You charge not in your spleen a noble person
And spoil your nobler soul: I say, take heed;
Yes, heartily beseech you.

If I know you correctly,
you were the Duke's surveyor, and lost your job
due to the complaints of the tenants: make sure
you do not out of anger lay charges on a noble person
and risk your immortal soul: be careful, I say;
yes, I am earnestly warning you.

KING HENRY VIII
Let him on.
Go forward.

Let him carry on.
Go on.

Surveyor
On my soul, I'll speak but truth.
I told my lord the duke, by the devil's illusions
The monk might be deceived; and that 'twas dangerous for him
To ruminate on this so far, until
It forged him some design, which, being believed,
It was much like to do: he answer'd, 'Tush,
It can do me no damage;' adding further,
That, had the king in his last sickness fail'd,
The cardinal's and Sir Thomas Lovell's heads
Should have gone off.

I swear on my soul I will only tell the truth.
I told my lord the Duke that the monk might be deceived
by tricks of the devil; and that it was dangerous for him
to think so much about this until
it made him take action, which, if he believed it,
it was very likely to do: he answered, 'Tosh,
it can do me no harm'; he further added
that if the king had died the last time he was ill,
Sir Thomas Lovell and the cardinal would have
lost their heads.

KING HENRY VIII
Ha! what, so rank? Ah ha!
There's mischief in this man: canst thou say further?

Ha! What, so evil? Aha!
There's mischief in this man: can you say anything else?

Surveyor
I can, my liege.

I can, my lord.

KING HENRY VIII
Proceed.

Go on.

Surveyor
Being at Greenwich,
After your highness had reproved the duke
About Sir William Blomer,--

When we were at Greenwich,

after your Highness had reproved the Duke
over Sir William Blomer–

KING HENRY VIII
I remember
Of such a time: being my sworn servant,
The duke retain'd him his. But on; what hence?

I remember
the incident: he was my sworn servant,
and the Duke employed him as his. But go on; what next?

Surveyor
'If,' quoth he, 'I for this had been committed,
As, to the Tower, I thought, I would have play'd
The part my father meant to act upon
The usurper Richard; who, being at Salisbury,
Made suit to come in's presence; which if granted,
As he made semblance of his duty, would
Have put his knife to him.'

'If,' he said, 'I had been, as I thought I was going
to be, sent to the Tower for this, I would have done
what my father meant to do to
the usurper Richard; when he was at Salisbury
he asked permission to see him; if he had granted it,
while he was pretending to do his duty he would have
stabbed him.'

KING HENRY VIII
A giant traitor!

A great traitor!

CARDINAL WOLSEY
Now, madam, may his highness live in freedom,
and this man out of prison?

Now, madam, may his Highness live in freedom,
with this man out of prison?

QUEEN KATHARINE
God mend all!

God save us all!

KING HENRY VIII
There's something more would out of thee; what say'st?

There's something more you want to say; what is it?

Surveyor
After 'the duke his father,' with 'the knife,'
He stretch'd him, and, with one hand on his dagger,
Another spread on's breast, mounting his eyes
He did discharge a horrible oath; whose tenor
Was,--were he evil used, he would outgo
His father by as much as a performance
Does an irresolute purpose.

After speaking of his father the Duke and the knife,
he stretched out and, with one hand on his dagger,
another one on his heart, he looked up
and swore a terrible oath; the substance of which
was that if he was badly treated he would outstrip
his father as much as doing outstrips weak planning.

KING HENRY VIII
There's his period,
To sheathe his knife in us. He is attach'd;
Call him to present trial: if he may
Find mercy in the law, 'tis his: if none,
Let him not seek 't of us: by day and night,
He's traitor to the height.

That's his plan,
to bury his knife in me. He's been arrested;
call him to trial at once: if he can
find mercy from the law, he may have it; if not,
don't let him look for it from me: by day and by night,
he's a terrible traitor.

Exeunt

SCENE III. An ante-chamber in the palace.

Enter Chamberlain and SANDS
Chamberlain
Is't possible the spells of France should juggle
Men into such strange mysteries?

Is it possible that the influence of France can make
men behave so strangely?

SANDS
New customs,
Though they be never so ridiculous,
Nay, let 'em be unmanly, yet are follow'd.

New customs,
however ridiculous they are,
even if they are unmanly, are always attractive.

Chamberlain
As far as I see, all the good our English
Have got by the late voyage is but merely
A fit or two o' the face; but they are shrewd ones;
For when they hold 'em, you would swear directly
Their very noses had been counsellors
To Pepin or Clotharius, they keep state so.

As far as I can see, the only good we English
have got from the recent expedition is just
some new grimaces; but they are clever,
for when they make them, you would certainly swear
that they had personally been counsellors
to Pepin or Clotharius, they give themselves such airs.

SANDS
They have all new legs, and lame ones: one would take it,
That never saw 'em pace before, the spavin
Or springhalt reign'd among 'em.

They all have new ways of walking, lame ways; one would believe,
if you had never seen them what before, that they had
some kind of disease of the legs.

Chamberlain
Death! my lord,
Their clothes are after such a pagan cut too,
That, sure, they've worn out Christendom.
Enter LOVELL
How now!
What news, Sir Thomas Lovell?

By God, my lord,
their clothes are also cut in such a pagan fashion
that you would think they were tired of Christianity.

Hello there!
What news, Sir Thomas Lovell?

LOVELL
Faith, my lord,
I hear of none, but the new proclamation
That's clapp'd upon the court-gate.

I swear, my lord,
I have heard nothing except the new proclamation
that has been put up on the palace gate.

Chamberlain
What is't for?

What does it say?

LOVELL
The reformation of our travell'd gallants,
That fill the court with quarrels, talk, and tailors.

It refers to the behaviour of our travelled noblemen,
who fill the court with quarrels, gossip and tailors.

Chamberlain
I'm glad 'tis there: now I would pray our monsieurs
To think an English courtier may be wise,
And never see the Louvre.

I'm glad this has been done: now I would hope these Frenchmen
will think an English courtier can be wise,
if he's never seen the Louvre.

LOVELL
They must either,
For so run the conditions, leave those remnants
Of fool and feather that they got in France,
With all their honourable point of ignorance
Pertaining thereunto, as fights and fireworks,
Abusing better men than they can be,
Out of a foreign wisdom, renouncing clean
The faith they have in tennis, and tall stockings,
Short blister'd breeches, and those types of travel,
And understand again like honest men;
Or pack to their old playfellows: there, I take it,
They may, 'cum privilegio,' wear away
The lag end of their lewdness and be laugh'd at.

The order says
that they must either abandon these foolish ways
of thinking and dressing that they picked up in France,
and all those silly habits associated
with them, such as fighting and fireworks,
abusing better men than they can hope to be
through their foreign wisdom, they must renounce at once
their delight in tennis, and long stockings,
short puffy breaches, and those marks of the travelled,
and behave again like honest men;
otherwise they can go back to their old playmates: there, I assume,
they can keep on with their behaviour without criticism
and while away their lasciviousness, and be laughed at.

SANDS
'Tis time to give 'em physic, their diseases
Are grown so catching.

It's time to give them medicine, their diseases
have become so infectious.

Chamberlain
What a loss our ladies
Will have of these trim vanities!

How much our ladies
will miss these fashionable fripperies!

LOVELL
Ay, marry,
There will be woe indeed, lords: the sly whoresons

Have got a speeding trick to lay down ladies;
A French song and a fiddle has no fellow.

Yes indeed
there will be sorrow, lords: the sly sons of bitches
are very good at seducing the ladies;
nothing can match a french song with a fiddle.

SANDS
The devil fiddle 'em! I am glad they are going,
For, sure, there's no converting of 'em: now
An honest country lord, as I am, beaten
A long time out of play, may bring his plainsong
And have an hour of hearing; and, by'r lady,
Held current music too.

May the devil fiddle with them! I'm glad they're going,
for there's certainly no way to convert them: now
an honest country lord like me, who's been pushed
out of the game for a long time, may try his plain song
and be listened to; and, by our Lady,
be thought of as fashionable.

Chamberlain
Well said, Lord Sands;
Your colt's tooth is not cast yet.

Well said, Lord Sands;
you haven't lost your youth yet.

SANDS
No, my lord;
Nor shall not, while I have a stump.

No, my lord;
and I shan't, while I have any of it left.

Chamberlain
Sir Thomas,
Whither were you a-going?

Sir Thomas,
where were you going?

LOVELL
To the cardinal's:

42

Your lordship is a guest too.

To the cardinal's:
your lordship is a guest too.

Chamberlain
O, 'tis true:
This night he makes a supper, and a great one,
To many lords and ladies; there will be
The beauty of this kingdom, I'll assure you.

Oh, that's true:
he's giving a great supper tonight
for many lords and ladies; all the
beauties of the kingdom will be there, I can assure you.

LOVELL
That churchman bears a bounteous mind indeed,
A hand as fruitful as the land that feeds us;
His dews fall every where.

That churchman has a generous mind indeed,
he is as bounteous as the land that feeds us;
he spreads his gifts far and wide.

Chamberlain
No doubt he's noble;
He had a black mouth that said other of him.

He's obviously a good man;
the one who spoke differently of him had a dirty mouth.

SANDS
He may, my lord; has wherewithal: in him
Sparing would show a worse sin than ill doctrine:
Men of his way should be most liberal;
They are set here for examples.

He did, my lord; he has the means: if he
was not generous it would be a worse sin than being
mistaken in his religion: men like him should be generous;
they are put on earth to be examples.

Chamberlain
True, they are so:
But few now give so great ones. My barge stays;

Your lordship shall along. Come, good Sir Thomas,
We shall be late else; which I would not be,
For I was spoke to, with Sir Henry Guildford
This night to be comptrollers.

It's true, they are:
but there are few who are so generous now. My barge is waiting;
your lordship shall come with me. Come, good Sir Thomas,
otherwise we will be late; I don't wish to be,
for I have been asked to be a steward tonight
along with Sir Henry Guildford.

SANDS
I am your lordship's.

I am at your lordship's service.

Exeunt

SCENE IV. A Hall in York Place.

Hautboys. A small table under a state for CARDINAL WOLSEY, a longer table for the guests.
Then enter ANNE and divers other Ladies and Gentlemen as guests, at one door; at another door,
enter GUILDFORD

GUILDFORD
Ladies, a general welcome from his grace
Salutes ye all; this night he dedicates
To fair content and you: none here, he hopes,
In all this noble bevy, has brought with her
One care abroad; he would have all as merry
As, first, good company, good wine, good welcome,
Can make good people. O, my lord, you're tardy:

Enter Chamberlain, SANDS, and LOVELL
The very thought of this fair company
Clapp'd wings to me.

Ladies, his grace sends a general welcome
to you all; he is dedicating tonight to
happiness and to you: he hopes that no one
in all of this noble group has brought with her
one worry from outside; he would like all to be as happy
as good company, good wine, and good welcome
can make good people. Oh, my lord, you're late:
just the thought of this beautiful company
made me hurry here.

Chamberlain
You are young, Sir Harry Guildford.

You are young, Sir Harry Guildford.

SANDS
Sir Thomas Lovell, had the cardinal
But half my lay thoughts in him, some of these
Should find a running banquet ere they rested,
I think would better please 'em: by my life,
They are a sweet society of fair ones.

Sir Thomas Lovell, if the cardinal

had only half of my layman's thoughts in him,
some of these would eat up quickly,
I think that would satisfy them: I swear,
this is a wonderful assembly of beautiful women.

LOVELL
O, that your lordship were but now confessor
To one or two of these!

Oh, if only your lordship was confessor
to one or two of these!

SANDS
I would I were;
They should find easy penance.

I wish I was;
their punishments would be easy.

LOVELL
Faith, how easy?

Tell us, how easy?

SANDS
As easy as a down-bed would afford it.

As easy as a feather bed could make them.

Chamberlain
Sweet ladies, will it please you sit? Sir Harry,
Place you that side; I'll take the charge of this:
His grace is entering. Nay, you must not freeze;
Two women placed together makes cold weather:
My Lord Sands, you are one will keep 'em waking;
Pray, sit between these ladies.

Sweet ladies, will you please sit down? Sir Harry,
you sit over there; I'll take charge of this side:
his Grace is coming. No, you mustn't sit together;
two women next to each other makes for a chilly time:
my Lord Sands, you will warm them up;
please, sit between these ladies.

SANDS
By my faith,

And thank your lordship. By your leave, sweet ladies:
If I chance to talk a little wild, forgive me;
I had it from my father.

I will indeed,
and I thank your lordship. With your permission, sweet ladies:
if I happen to talk a little wildly, forgive me;
I inherited the habit from my father.

ANNE
Was he mad, sir?

Was he mad, sir?

SANDS
O, very mad, exceeding mad, in love too:
But he would bite none; just as I do now,
He would kiss you twenty with a breath.

Oh, very mad, exceedingly mad, mad in love too:
but he never bit anyone; he would kiss
twenty of you in an instant, just as I do now.

Kisses her

Chamberlain
Well said, my lord.
So, now you're fairly seated. Gentlemen,
The penance lies on you, if these fair ladies
Pass away frowning.

Well said, my lord.
So, now everyone is seated. Gentlemen,
you will be to blame, if these fair ladies
leave without smiles on their faces.

SANDS
For my little cure,
Let me alone.

You can trust me
with my share.

Hautboys. Enter CARDINAL WOLSEY, and takes his state

CARDINAL WOLSEY

You're welcome, my fair guests: that noble lady,
Or gentleman, that is not freely merry,
Is not my friend: this, to confirm my welcome;
And to you all, good health.

You are welcome, my fair guests: any noble lady,
or gentleman, who is not openly happy
is not my friend: I toast you to confirm my welcome;
and I wish you all good health.

Drinks

SANDS
Your grace is noble:
Let me have such a bowl may hold my thanks,
And save me so much talking.

Your grace is noble:
let me have a cup big enough to show my thanks,
and save me having to speak.

CARDINAL WOLSEY
My Lord Sands,
I am beholding to you: cheer your neighbours.
Ladies, you are not merry: gentlemen,
Whose fault is this?

My Lord Sands,
I am indebted to you: cheer up your neighbours.
Ladies, you are not jolly: gentlemen,
whose fault is this?

SANDS
The red wine first must rise
In their fair cheeks, my lord; then we shall have 'em
Talk us to silence.

We must let the wine redden
their fair cheeks first, my lord; then they shall
talk us into silence.

ANNE
You are a merry gamester,
My Lord Sands.

You are cheerful joker,

my Lord Sands.

SANDS
Yes, if I make my play.
Here's to your ladyship: and pledge it, madam,
For 'tis to such a thing,--

Yes, when I'm allowed to be.
I drink to your ladyship: and match it, madam,
for I'm drinking to something–

ANNE
You cannot show me.

Which you cannot show me.

SANDS
I told your grace they would talk anon.

I told your grace they would talk soon enough.

Drum and trumpet, chambers discharged

CARDINAL WOLSEY
What's that?

What's that?

Chamberlain
Look out there, some of ye.

Look outside, some of you.

Exit Servant

CARDINAL WOLSEY
What warlike voice,
And to what end is this? Nay, ladies, fear not;
By all the laws of war you're privileged.

What's the meaning of this
warlike noise? Do not be afraid, ladies;
you are exempt by all the laws of war.

Re-enter Servant

Chamberlain
How now! what is't?

Hello there! What is it?

Servant
A noble troop of strangers;
For so they seem: they've left their barge and landed;
And hither make, as great ambassadors
From foreign princes.

A noble band of foreigners;
that's what they look like: they have left their barge and landed;
and they are coming here, like great ambassadors
from foreign princes.

CARDINAL WOLSEY
Good lord chamberlain,
Go, give 'em welcome; you can speak the French tongue;
And, pray, receive 'em nobly, and conduct 'em
Into our presence, where this heaven of beauty
Shall shine at full upon them. Some attend him.
Exit Chamberlain, attended. All rise, and tables removed
You have now a broken banquet; but we'll mend it.
A good digestion to you all: and once more
I shower a welcome on ye; welcome all.
Hautboys. Enter KING HENRY VIII and others, as masquers, habited like shepherds, ushered by
the Chamberlain. They pass directly before CARDINAL WOLSEY, and gracefully salute him
A noble company! what are their pleasures?

Good Lord Chamberlain,
go and welcome them; you can speak French;
and please, give them a noble welcome, and bring them
here to me, where they can enjoy the sight
of all this heavenly beauty. Some of you go with him.

The banquet has been disturbed, but we shall make up for it.
May you all digest your food well, and once more
I give you all my best welcome.

This is a noble company! What would you like?

Chamberlain
Because they speak no English, thus they pray'd
To tell your grace, that, having heard by fame
Of this so noble and so fair assembly

This night to meet here, they could do no less
Out of the great respect they bear to beauty,
But leave their flocks; and, under your fair conduct,
Crave leave to view these ladies and entreat
An hour of revels with 'em.

Because they speak no English, they begged me
to tell your grace, that, having heard by reputation
that such a noble and beautiful assembly
was going to be here tonight, they couldn't do any less,
out of the great respect they have for beauty,
than leave their flocks; and, with your kind permission,
they beg that they can see these ladies and ask
them to dance with them for an hour.

CARDINAL WOLSEY
Say, lord chamberlain,
They have done my poor house grace; for which I pay 'em
A thousand thanks, and pray 'em take their pleasures.

Tell them, Lord Chamberlain,
that they are honouring my poor house; I give them
a thousand thanks for that, and ask them to choose whom they want.

They choose Ladies for the dance. KING HENRY VIII chooses ANNE

KING HENRY VIII
The fairest hand I ever touch'd! O beauty,
Till now I never knew thee!

The loveliest hand I ever touched! O beauty,
I never knew you until now!

Music. Dance

CARDINAL WOLSEY
My lord!

My lord!

Chamberlain
Your grace?

Your Grace?

CARDINAL WOLSEY

Pray, tell 'em thus much from me:
There should be one amongst 'em, by his person,
More worthy this place than myself; to whom,
If I but knew him, with my love and duty
I would surrender it.

Please tell them this from me:
that there should be someone amongst them who,
through his position, is more worthy of this place than me;
if I knew who he was my love and duty
would make me give it to him.

Chamberlain
I will, my lord.

I will, my lord.

Whispers the Masquers

CARDINAL WOLSEY
What say they?

What do they say?

Chamberlain
Such a one, they all confess,
There is indeed; which they would have your grace
Find out, and he will take it.

They all admit that there is such a person,
and he will take your place if your Grace
can discover who it is.

CARDINAL WOLSEY
Let me see, then.
By all your good leaves, gentlemen; here I'll make
My royal choice.

Let me see, then.
If you will excuse me, gentlemen; I choose
this one as being royal.

KING HENRY VIII
Ye have found him, cardinal:
Unmasking
You hold a fair assembly; you do well, lord:

You are a churchman, or, I'll tell you, cardinal,
I should judge now unhappily.

You have found him, cardinal:

you are hosting a beautiful assembly; you are doing well, lord:
I'll tell you, cardinal, if you weren't a churchman
I might judge you unfavourably.

CARDINAL WOLSEY
I am glad
Your grace is grown so pleasant.

I am glad
that your Grace is so merry.

KING HENRY VIII
My lord chamberlain,
Prithee, come hither: what fair lady's that?

My lord chamberlain,
please, come here: who is that beautiful lady?

Chamberlain
An't please your grace, Sir Thomas Bullen's daughter--
The Viscount Rochford,--one of her highness' women.

If you please, your Grace, that is Sir Thomas Bullen's daughter--
the Viscount Rochford--one of her Highness' waiting ladies.

KING HENRY VIII
By heaven, she is a dainty one. Sweetheart,
I were unmannerly, to take you out,
And not to kiss you. A health, gentlemen!
Let it go round.

By heaven, she's a dainty one. Sweetheart,
I would be ill mannered to choose you
and not to kiss you. Good health, gentlemen!
Pass it round.

CARDINAL WOLSEY
Sir Thomas Lovell, is the banquet ready
I' the privy chamber?

Sir Thomas Lovell, is the banquet ready

in the next room?

LOVELL
Yes, my lord.

Yes, my lord.

CARDINAL WOLSEY
Your grace,
I fear, with dancing is a little heated.

I fear your Grace
has become a little hot from dancing.

KING HENRY VIII
I fear, too much.

Too much, I fear.

CARDINAL WOLSEY
There's fresher air, my lord,
In the next chamber.

The air is cooler, my lord,
in the next room.

KING HENRY VIII
Lead in your ladies, every one: sweet partner,
I must not yet forsake you: let's be merry:
Good my lord cardinal, I have half a dozen healths
To drink to these fair ladies, and a measure
To lead 'em once again; and then let's dream
Who's best in favour. Let the music knock it.

Bring in your ladies, everyone: sweet partner,
I must not leave you yet: let's be jolly:
my good lord cardinal, I have half a dozen healths
to drink to these fair ladies, and another dance
to have with them; and then let's dream
of the most beautiful. Strike up the music.

Exeunt with trumpets

Act II

SCENE I. Westminster. A street.

Enter two Gentlemen, meeting
First Gentleman
Whither away so fast?

Where are you going so quickly?

Second Gentleman
O, God save ye!
Even to the hall, to hear what shall become
Of the great Duke of Buckingham.

Oh, God bless you!
I'm going to the hall, to hear what will happen
to the great Duke of Buckingham.

First Gentleman
I'll save you
That labour, sir. All's now done, but the ceremony
Of bringing back the prisoner.

I'll save you
the bother, sir. Everything is finished, except for the ceremony
of bringing back the prisoner.

Second Gentleman
Were you there?

Were you there?

First Gentleman
Yes, indeed, was I.

Yes indeed I was.

Second Gentleman
Pray, speak what has happen'd.

Please, tell me what happened.

First Gentleman

You may guess quickly what.

You can easily guess that.

Second Gentleman
Is he found guilty?

Has he been found guilty?

First Gentleman
Yes, truly is he, and condemn'd upon't.

He certainly has, and condemned to death for it.

Second Gentleman
I am sorry for't.

I'm sorry to hear it.

First Gentleman
So are a number more.

So are several others.

Second Gentleman
But, pray, how pass'd it?

But, please, what happened?

First Gentleman
I'll tell you in a little. The great duke
Came to the bar; where to his accusations
He pleaded still not guilty and alleged
Many sharp reasons to defeat the law.
The king's attorney on the contrary
Urged on the examinations, proofs, confessions
Of divers witnesses; which the duke desired
To have brought viva voce to his face:
At which appear'd against him his surveyor;
Sir Gilbert Peck his chancellor; and John Car,
Confessor to him; with that devil-monk,
Hopkins, that made this mischief.

*I can tell you briefly. The great Duke
was brought to the court; he pleaded not guilty
to the accusations and gave*

many good reasons in his defence.
Against him the King's attorney
emphasised the interrogations, proofs and confessions
of several witnesses; the Duke wanted
them to be brought to give evidence to his face:
at that point his surveyor appeared against him;
so did Gilbert Peck, his Chancellor; and John Car,
his confessor; along with that devilish monk
Hopkins, who started all this mischief.

Second Gentleman
That was he
That fed him with his prophecies?

The one who
stuffed him with prophecies?

First Gentleman
The same.
All these accused him strongly; which he fain
Would have flung from him, but, indeed, he could not:
And so his peers, upon this evidence,
Have found him guilty of high treason. Much
He spoke, and learnedly, for life; but all
Was either pitied in him or forgotten.

That's him.
They all made strong accusations against him;
he tried to reject them, but, in fact, he couldn't:
and so his peers, looking at the evidence,
have found him guilty of high treason. He made
a long and learned speech for his life; but everything
he said either had no effect or just made them pity him.

Second Gentleman
After all this, how did he bear himself?

After all this, how did he conduct himself?

First Gentleman
When he was brought again to the bar, to hear
His knell rung out, his judgment, he was stirr'd
With such an agony, he sweat extremely,
And something spoke in choler, ill, and hasty:
But he fell to himself again, and sweetly
In all the rest show'd a most noble patience.

When he was brought back to the bar, to hear
the death bell of his sentence, he was agitated
by such agony, he sweated a great deal,
and said something in anger, bad and hasty:
but he soon became himself again, and in
everything else he showed a sweet and noble calm.

Second Gentleman
I do not think he fears death.

I don't think he's afraid of death.

First Gentleman
Sure, he does not:
He never was so womanish; the cause
He may a little grieve at.

He certainly doesn't;
he was never so effeminate; he may be
a little upset by the cause of it.

Second Gentleman
Certainly
The cardinal is the end of this.

Certainly
the cardinal is at the bottom of this.

First Gentleman
'Tis likely,
By all conjectures: first, Kildare's attainder,
Then deputy of Ireland; who removed,
Earl Surrey was sent thither, and in haste too,
Lest he should help his father.

Everything
points to it: firstly, Kildare losing his
position as deputy of Ireland; when he was removed
the Earl of Surrey was sent there, and quickly too,
in case he should help his father.

Second Gentleman
That trick of state
Was a deep envious one.

That political trick
was a cunning and malicious one.

First Gentleman
At his return
No doubt he will requite it. This is noted,
And generally, whoever the king favours,
The cardinal instantly will find employment,
And far enough from court too.

No doubt he will
repay it when he comes back. Everybody has
noticed that whenever the King favours someone
the cardinal will instantly find him a job
far away from the court.

Second Gentleman
All the commons
Hate him perniciously, and, o' my conscience,
Wish him ten fathom deep: this duke as much
They love and dote on; call him bounteous Buckingham,
The mirror of all courtesy;--

All the common people
hate him deeply, and, I swear,
wish he was drowned ten fathoms down: they love
and esteem this duke just as much; they call him bounteous Buckingham,
the image of courtesy;

First Gentleman
Stay there, sir,
And see the noble ruin'd man you speak of.

Wait there, Sir,
and see the ruined nobleman you speak of.

Enter BUCKINGHAM from his arraignment; tip-staves before him; the axe with the edge towards him; halberds on each side: accompanied with LOVELL, VAUX, SANDS, and common people

Second Gentleman
Let's stand close, and behold him.

Let's stand nearby, and watch him.

BUCKINGHAM
All good people,

You that thus far have come to pity me,
Hear what I say, and then go home and lose me.
I have this day received a traitor's judgment,
And by that name must die: yet, heaven bear witness,
And if I have a co nscience, let it sink me,
Even as the axe falls, if I be not faithful!
The law I bear no malice for my death;
'T has done, upon the premises, but justice:
But those that sought it I could wish more Christians:
Be what they will, I heartily forgive 'em:
Yet let 'em look they glory not in mischief,
Nor build their evils on the graves of great men;
For then my guiltless blood must cry against 'em.
For further life in this world I ne'er hope,
Nor will I sue, although the king have mercies
More than I dare make faults. You few that loved me,
And dare be bold to weep for Buckingham,
His noble friends and fellows, whom to leave
Is only bitter to him, only dying,
Go with me, like good angels, to my end;
And, as the long divorce of steel falls on me,
Make of your prayers one sweet sacrifice,
And lift my soul to heaven. Lead on, o' God's name.

All you good people,
you who have come so far to show your pity for me,
hear what I have to say, and then go home and forget about me.
I have been adjudged to be a traitor today,
and must die with that name; but as heaven is my witness,
and if I have a conscience, let it destroy me,
even as the axe falls, if I am not faithful.
I have nothing against the law for my death,
the forms of justice were followed:
but those who wanted me dead, I wish they were more Christian:
whatever they are, I heartily forgive them;
but let them make sure they do not glory in mischief,
nor use the graves of great men as foundations for their evils,
for then my guiltless blood will cry out against them.
I do not hope for any more life in this world,
and I will not beg, although the King has more mercy
than I have committed offences. You few who loved me,
and are brave enough to weep for Buckingham,
my noble friends and companions, whom having to leave
is my only cause of bitterness, my only death;
come with me to my end like good angels,
and as the steel sword falls upon me,

make a great offering of your prayers
to lift my soul to heaven. Lead on in God's name.

LOVELL
I do beseech your grace, for charity,
If ever any malice in your heart
Were hid against me, now to forgive me frankly.

I must beg your grace, out of kindness,
that if there was ever any malice hidden in your heart
against me, openly forgive me.

BUCKINGHAM
Sir Thomas Lovell, I as free forgive you
As I would be forgiven: I forgive all;
There cannot be those numberless offences
'Gainst me, that I cannot take peace with:
no black envy
Shall mark my grave. Commend me to his grace;
And if he speak of Buckingham, pray, tell him
You met him half in heaven: my vows and prayers
Yet are the king's; and, till my soul forsake,
Shall cry for blessings on him: may he live
Longer than I have time to tell his years!
Ever beloved and loving may his rule be!
And when old time shall lead him to his end,
Goodness and he fill up one monument!

Sir Thomas Lovell, I forgive you as freely
as I would like to be forgiven: I forgive everyone;
I will not have any offences against me
of that kind, I will make truce with everyone:
no black envy will hang over my grave.
Give his grace my compliments;
and if he talks of Buckingham, please tell him
when you saw him he was halfway to Heaven: my vows and my prayers
are still with the king; and, until my soul departs,
I shall ask for blessings on him: may he live
for longer than I have time now to count his years;
May his reign always be loving and beloved;
and when he finally reaches the end of his days,
may he and goodness share the same grave!

LOVELL
To the water side I must conduct your grace;
Then give my charge up to Sir Nicholas Vaux,

Who undertakes you to your end.

I must escort your Grace to the waterside;
then I must hand responsibility over to Sir Nicholas Vaux,
who will take you to your end.

VAUX
Prepare there,
The duke is coming: see the barge be ready;
And fit it with such furniture as suits
The greatness of his person.

Get ready,
the Duke is coming: make sure the barge is prepared;
and put furniture in it which suits
his great nobility.

BUCKINGHAM
Nay, Sir Nicholas,
Let it alone; my state now will but mock me.
When I came hither, I was lord high constable
And Duke of Buckingham; now, poor Edward Bohun:
Yet I am richer than my base accusers,
That never knew what truth meant: I now seal it;
And with that blood will make 'em one day groan for't.
My noble father, Henry of Buckingham,
Who first raised head against usurping Richard,
Flying for succor to his servant Banister,
Being distress'd, was by that wretch betray'd,
And without trial fell; God's peace be with him!
Henry the Seventh succeeding, truly pitying
My father's loss, like a most royal prince,
Restored me to my honours, and, out of ruins,
Made my name once more noble. Now his son,
Henry the Eighth, life, honour, name and all
That made me happy at one stroke has taken
For ever from the world. I had my trial,
And, must needs say, a noble one; which makes me,
A little happier than my wretched father:
Yet thus far we are one in fortunes: both
Fell by our servants, by those men we loved most;
A most unnatural and faithless service!
Heaven has an end in all: yet, you that hear me,
This from a dying man receive as certain:
Where you are liberal of your loves and counsels
Be sure you be not loose; for those you make friends

And give your hearts to, when they once perceive
The least rub in your fortunes, fall away
Like water from ye, never found again
But where they mean to sink ye. All good people,
Pray for me! I must now forsake ye: the last hour
Of my long weary life is come upon me. Farewell:
And when you would say something that is sad,
Speak how I fell. I have done; and God forgive me!

No, Sir Nicholas,
let it be; my position would just mock me now.
When I came here I was Lord High Constable
and Duke of Buckingham: now I am poor Edward Bohun;
but I am richer than my low accusers,
who never knew what truth meant: I shall now prove it
with the blood price which one day they will suffer for.
My noble father Henry of Buckingham,
the first one to raise forces against usurping Richard,
running for assistance to his servant Banister,
when he was in need, was betrayed by that wretch,
and executed without trial; may God's peace be upon him.
Henry the Seventh succeeded, and as he truly pitied
the loss of my father, he gave me back my titles
like the Royal Prince he was; and out of the ruins
he reinstated my noble name. Now his son,
Henry the Eighth, in one blow has taken away
my life, honour, title and everything
that made me happy. I had my trial,
and I have to say it was a noble one; that makes me
a little happier than my wretched father:
but we are identical in one way; we were both
brought down by our servants, by those men we loved most:
very unnatural and faithless service.
Heaven always has a purpose; but you who hear me,
take this as the truth from a dying man:
when you are generous with your love and advice,
make sure you are not profligate; for those you have as friends
and give your hearts to, as soon as they see
that your fortunes are failing, they shall drop away from you
like water, you'll never see them again
until they try to drown you. Pray for me,
all good people; now I must leave you; the last hour
of my long weary life has come:
farewell; and when you want to speak about something that's sad,
talk of my end. I have finished, and may God forgive me.

Exeunt BUCKINGHAM and Train

First Gentleman
O, this is full of pity! Sir, it calls,
I fear, too many curses on their heads
That were the authors.

Oh, this is pitiable! Sir, I fear
it brings down too many curses on the heads
of those who are responsible.

Second Gentleman
If the duke be guiltless,
'Tis full of woe: yet I can give you inkling
Of an ensuing evil, if it fall,
Greater than this.

If the Duke is not guilty,
it's very sad: but I can give you a hint
of an even greater evil that is
coming, if it happens.

First Gentleman
Good angels keep it from us!
What may it be? You do not doubt my faith, sir?

May the good angels keep it from us!
What is it? You don't doubt my loyalty, sir?

Second Gentleman
This secret is so weighty, 'twill require
A strong faith to conceal it.

This secret is so great, it will need
great loyalty to keep it hidden.

First Gentleman
Let me have it;
I do not talk much.

Tell me;
I don't talk much.

Second Gentleman
I am confident,
You shall, sir: did you not of late days hear

A buzzing of a separation
Between the king and Katharine?

I trust you,
I shall tell you: haven't you recently heard
gossip about a divorce
between the King and Katherine?

First Gentleman
Yes, but it held not:
For when the king once heard it, out of anger
He sent command to the lord mayor straight
To stop the rumor, and allay those tongues
That durst disperse it.

Yes, but it didn't last:
for as soon as the King heard of it he angrily
sent orders at once to the Lord Mayor
to stop the rumour, and control the people
who were spreading it.

Second Gentleman
But that slander, sir,
Is found a truth now: for it grows again
Fresher than e'er it was; and held for certain
The king will venture at it. Either the cardinal,
Or some about him near, have, out of malice
To the good queen, possess'd him with a scruple
That will undo her: to confirm this too,
Cardinal Campeius is arrived, and lately;
As all think, for this business.

But that slander, Sir,
is now proved to be true: it's sprung up again
stronger than it ever was; and it is thought certain
that the King will do it. Either the cardinal,
or someone else close to him, has, out of malice
towards the good Queen, placed doubts in him
that will be her downfall: to confirm this,
Cardinal Campeius has recently arrived;
everyone thinks it's to do with this affair.

First Gentleman
'Tis the cardinal;
And merely to revenge him on the emperor
For not bestowing on him, at his asking,

The archbishopric of Toledo, this is purposed.

It is the cardinal;
and he will agree to act in this matter
just to take revenge on the Emperor
for not giving him the archbishopric of Toledo
when he asked for it.

Second Gentleman
I think you have hit the mark: but is't not cruel
That she should feel the smart of this? The cardinal
Will have his will, and she must fall.

I think you've hit the nail on the head: but isn't it cruel
that the Queen should suffer for this? The cardinal
will get what he wants, and she must fall.

First Gentleman
'Tis woful.
We are too open here to argue this;
Let's think in private more.

It's woeful,
we are too exposed to talk about this here;
let's discuss it more privately.

Exeunt

SCENE II. An ante-chamber in the palace.

Enter Chamberlain, reading a letter

Chamberlain
'My lord, the horses your lordship sent for, with
all the care I had, I saw well chosen, ridden, and
furnished. They were young and handsome, and of the
best breed in the north. When they were ready to
set out for London, a man of my lord cardinal's, by
commission and main power, took 'em from me; with
this reason: His master would be served before a
subject, if not before the king; which stopped our
mouths, sir.'
I fear he will indeed: well, let him have them:
He will have all, I think.

'My Lord, the horses your lordship sent for have been
chosen, trained and saddled with my very best care.
They were young and handsome, and from the
best breed in the north. When they were ready to
be sent to London, a man of my lord cardinal's
took them from me with his authority and by brute force;
he gave this reason: if his master was not served before the king,
he would at least be served before a subject; and that
stopped us arguing, sir.'
I'm afraid he certainly will; well, let him have them;
I think he will have everything.

Enter, to Chamberlain, NORFOLK and SUFFOLK

NORFOLK
Well met, my lord chamberlain.

Good to see you, my lord chamberlain.

Chamberlain
Good day to both your graces.

Good day to both your graces.

SUFFOLK

68

How is the king employ'd?

What is the king doing?

Chamberlain
I left him private,
Full of sad thoughts and troubles.

I left him sitting alone,
full of sad thoughts and troubles.

NORFOLK
What's the cause?

For what reason?

Chamberlain
It seems the marriage with his brother's wife
Has crept too near his conscience.

It seems he is feeling bad about
marrying his brother's wife.

SUFFOLK
No, his conscience
Has crept too near another lady.

No, he's feeling bad
about not being with a different lady.

NORFOLK
'Tis so:
This is the cardinal's doing, the king-cardinal:
That blind priest, like the eldest son of fortune,
Turns what he list. The king will know him one day.

That's right:
this is the cardinal's doing, the king-cardinal:
that man is like fate, he doesn't care who he
makes suffer. The king shall find him out one day.

SUFFOLK
Pray God he do! he'll never know himself else.

I pray to God he does! Otherwise he will never know himself.

NORFOLK
How holily he works in all his business!
And with what zeal! for, now he has crack'd the league
Between us and the emperor, the queen's great nephew,
He dives into the king's soul, and there scatters
Dangers, doubts, wringing of the conscience,
Fears, and despairs; and all these for his marriage:
And out of all these to restore the king,
He counsels a divorce; a loss of her
That, like a jewel, has hung twenty years
About his neck, yet never lost her lustre;
Of her that loves him with that excellence
That angels love good men with; even of her
That, when the greatest stroke of fortune falls,
Will bless the king: and is not this course pious?

With what holiness he goes about his business!
How keen he is! for, now he has broken the alliance
between us and the Emperor, the great-nephew of the Queen,
he plunges into the soul of the King, and scatters about
fears, doubts, torment to his conscience,
despair; and always on account of his marriage:
and to save the King from these,
he advises divorce; throwing away her
who has hung around his neck like a jewel
for twenty years and never lost her shine;
someone who loves him with the purity
with which angels love good men; even
when the axe falls upon her she will
bless the King: is this holy behaviour?

Chamberlain
Heaven keep me from such counsel! 'Tis most true
These news are every where; every tongue speaks 'em,
And every true heart weeps for't: all that dare
Look into these affairs see this main end,
The French king's sister. Heaven will one day open
The king's eyes, that so long have slept upon
This bold bad man.

May heaven protect me from such advice! It's true
that this news is everywhere; everybody speaking about it,
and every true heart is weeping for it: everyone who dares
look into these affairs see the main purpose
is to get the sister of the French king. One day heaven will open
the eyes of the King, that have for so long been blind

to the badness of this bold man.

SUFFOLK
And free us from his slavery.

And free us from his slavery.

NORFOLK
We had need pray,
And heartily, for our deliverance;
Or this imperious man will work us all
From princes into pages: all men's honours
Lie like one lump before him, to be fashion'd
Into what pitch he please.

We must pray,
and heartily, to be saved from him;
or this arrogant man will turn us all
from Princes into servants: all the honours of men
lie in front of him like one big lump of clay, to be shaped
into anything he fancies.

SUFFOLK
For me, my lords,
I love him not, nor fear him; there's my creed:
As I am made without him, so I'll stand,
If the king please; his curses and his blessings
Touch me alike, they're breath I not believe in.
I knew him, and I know him; so I leave him
To him that made him proud, the pope.

For me, my lords,
I do not love him, nor do I fear him; this is what I believe:
as I do not owe him my position I shall stand firm,
if the King pleases; his curses and his blessings
are the same to me, I don't believe in either of them.
I knew him, and I know what he's like; and so I leave him
to the one who gave him his position, the Pope.

NORFOLK
Let's in;
And with some other business put the king
From these sad thoughts, that work too much upon him:
My lord, you'll bear us company?

Let's go indoors;

let's think about something else rather than
the sad business of the King, which we think about too much:
my lord, will you come with us?

Chamberlain
Excuse me;
The king has sent me otherwhere: besides,
You'll find a most unfit time to disturb him:
Health to your lordships.

Pardon me;
the King has sent me somewhere else: anyway,
you will find this is a very bad time to disturb him:
good health to your Lordships.

NORFOLK
Thanks, my good lord chamberlain.

Thank you, my good Lord Chamberlain.

Exit Chamberlain; and KING HENRY VIII draws the curtain, and sits reading pensively

SUFFOLK
How sad he looks! sure, he is much afflicted.

How sad he looks! He certainly is much affected.

KING HENRY VIII
Who's there, ha?

Who's there, hey?

NORFOLK
Pray God he be not angry.

Please God don't let him be angry.

KING HENRY VIII
Who's there, I say? How dare you thrust yourselves
Into my private meditations?
Who am I? ha?

Who's there, I say? How dare you barge in
on my private thoughts?
Who am I? Hey?

NORFOLK
A gracious king that pardons all offences
Malice ne'er meant: our breach of duty this way
Is business of estate; in which we come
To know your royal pleasure.

You are gracious king who pardons all offences
that were not meant in malice: we are only disturbing you
with matters of state; we have come
to take your royal orders.

KING HENRY VIII
Ye are too bold:
Go to; I'll make ye know your times of business:
Is this an hour for temporal affairs, ha?
Enter CARDINAL WOLSEY and CARDINAL CAMPEIUS, with a commission
Who's there? my good lord cardinal? O my Wolsey,
The quiet of my wounded conscience;
Thou art a cure fit for a king.
To CARDINAL CAMPEIUS
You're welcome,
Most learned reverend sir, into our kingdom:
Use us and it.
To CARDINAL WOLSEY
My good lord, have great care
I be not found a talker.

You are too cheeky:
go away; I'll teach you when business hours are:
is this the time for earthly affairs, hey?
[To Cardinal Wolsey]
Who's there? My good lord cardinal? Oh my Wolsey,
the cure for my wounded conscience;
you are a cure fit for a king.
[To Cardinal Campeius]
You are welcome,
most learned and respected sir, to my kingdom;
I and it are at your service.
[To Cardinal Wolsey]
Make sure I don't break these promises.

CARDINAL WOLSEY
Sir, you cannot.
I would your grace would give us but an hour
Of private conference.

Sir, you couldn't.
I should like your grace to give us just an hour
for private discussion.

KING HENRY VIII
[To NORFOLK and SUFFOLK]
We are busy; go.

We are busy; go.

NORFOLK
[Aside to SUFFOLK]
This priest has no pride in him?

Has this priest any pride?

SUFFOLK
[Aside to NORFOLK] Not to speak of:
I would not be so sick though for his place:
But this cannot continue.

None to speak of:
but I would not be sick with pride in his place:
but this cannot carry on.

NORFOLK
[Aside to SUFFOLK] If it do,
I'll venture one have-at-him.

If it does,
I'll take a bash at him.

SUFFOLK
[Aside to NORFOLK] I another.

Me too.

Exeunt NORFOLK and SUFFOLK

CARDINAL WOLSEY
Your grace has given a precedent of wisdom
Above all princes, in committing freely
Your scruple to the voice of Christendom:
Who can be angry now? what envy reach you?
The Spaniard, tied blood and favour to her,
Must now confess, if they have any goodness,

The trial just and noble. All the clerks,
I mean the learned ones, in Christian kingdoms
Have their free voices: Rome, the nurse of judgment,
Invited by your noble self, hath sent
One general tongue unto us, this good man,
This just and learned priest, Cardinal Campeius;
Whom once more I present unto your highness.

Your Grace has given an example of wisdom
greater than all Princes, in freely submitting
your doubts to the voice of Christendom:
who can be angry now? Who can criticise you?
The Emperor, tied to her through blood and friendship,
must now admit, if he has any goodness,
that the trial was fair and noble. All the clerks,
I mean the ones of great learning, in Christian kingdoms
have given their free opinions: Rome, the seat of judgement,
has, invited by yourself, sent us their mouthpiece,
this good man, this just and learned priest, Cardinal Campeius;
I once again present him to your Highness.

KING HENRY VIII
And once more in mine arms I bid him welcome,
And thank the holy conclave for their loves:
They have sent me such a man I would have wish'd for.

And once more I hug him in welcome,
and thank the school of Cardinals for their love:
they have sent me just such a man as I would wish for.

CARDINAL CAMPEIUS
Your grace must needs deserve all strangers' loves,
You are so noble. To your highness' hand
I tender my commission; by whose virtue,
The court of Rome commanding, you, my lord
Cardinal of York, are join'd with me their servant
In the unpartial judging of this business.

Your Grace deserves the love of all foreigners,
you are so noble. I hand over my orders
to your Highness' hand; they demand in the name
of the court of Rome that you, my lord
Cardinal of York, should join with me, their servant,
in an impartial judging of this business.

KING HENRY VIII

Two equal men. The queen shall be acquainted
Forthwith for what you come. Where's Gardiner?

Two equally great men. The Queen shall be told
at once why you have come. Where's Gardiner?

CARDINAL WOLSEY
I know your majesty has always loved her
So dear in heart, not to deny her that
A woman of less place might ask by law:
Scholars allow'd freely to argue for her.

I know your Majesty has always loved her
so very dearly that you will not deny her
what a less favoured woman might lawfully ask for:
scholars allowed to put forward their arguments for her freely.

KING HENRY VIII
Ay, and the best she shall have; and my favour
To him that does best: God forbid else. Cardinal,
Prithee, call Gardiner to me, my new secretary:
I find him a fit fellow.

Yes, and she shall have the best; and I shall treat
the one who does best well: God forbid otherwise. Cardinal,
please, call Gardiner, my new secretary, to me:
I find him a good man.

Exit CARDINAL WOLSEY
Re-enter CARDINAL WOLSEY, with GARDINER

CARDINAL WOLSEY
[Aside to GARDINER] Give me your hand: much joy and
favour to you;
You are the king's now.

Give me your hand: much joy and good fortune to you;
you now work for the King.

GARDINER
[Aside to CARDINAL WOLSEY]
But to be commanded
For ever by your grace, whose hand has raised me.

But I will always be at the orders
of your grace, who gave me this position.

KING HENRY VIII
Come hither, Gardiner.

Come here, Gardiner.

Walks and whispers

CARDINAL CAMPEIUS
My Lord of York, was not one Doctor Pace
In this man's place before him?

My Lord of York, wasn't there someone called Doctor Pace
in this man's position before?

CARDINAL WOLSEY
Yes, he was.

Yes, there was.

CARDINAL CAMPEIUS
Was he not held a learned man?

Wasn't he thought of as a learned man?

CARDINAL WOLSEY
Yes, surely.

He certainly was.

CARDINAL CAMPEIUS
Believe me, there's an ill opinion spread then
Even of yourself, lord cardinal.

Then believe me, there is malicious gossip
about yourself, Lord Cardinal.

CARDINAL WOLSEY
How! of me?

What! About me?

CARDINAL CAMPEIUS
They will not stick to say you envied him,
And fearing he would rise, he was so virtuous,
Kept him a foreign man still; which so grieved him,

That he ran mad and died.

They won't stop saying that you envied him,
and because you feared he would be promoted, as he was so good,
you kept him away from the court; and that made him so sad
that he went mad and died.

CARDINAL WOLSEY
Heaven's peace be with him!
That's Christian care enough: for living murmurers
There's places of rebuke. He was a fool;
For he would needs be virtuous: that good fellow,
If I command him, follows my appointment:
I will have none so near else. Learn this, brother,
We live not to be grip'd by meaner persons.

May he rest in peace!
That's enough Christian care: for living gossips
there are ways of punishing them. He was a fool;
he insisted on being good: that good fellow,
if I command him, does as I say:
I won't have anyone else this close. Remember this, brother,
we're not here for low people to be familiar with.

KING HENRY VIII
Deliver this with modesty to the queen.
Exit GARDINER
The most convenient place that I can think of
For such receipt of learning is Black-Friars;
There ye shall meet about this weighty business.
My Wolsey, see it furnish'd. O, my lord,
Would it not grieve an able man to leave
So sweet a bedfellow? But, conscience, conscience!
O, 'tis a tender place; and I must leave her.

Convey this politely to the Queen.
The best place I can think of
to discuss such learning is Blackfriars;
that's where you shall meet to discuss this weighty matter.
My Wolsey, see that it is furnished. Oh, my lord,
wouldn't it make an able man sorrowful to have to leave
such a sweet bedmate? But, there is conscience!
It is tender, and I must leave her.

Exeunt

SCENE III. An ante-chamber of the QUEEN'S apartments.

Enter ANNE and an Old Lady

ANNE
Not for that neither: here's the pang that pinches:
His highness having lived so long with her, and she
So good a lady that no tongue could ever
Pronounce dishonour of her; by my life,
She never knew harm-doing: O, now, after
So many courses of the sun enthroned,
Still growing in a majesty and pomp, the which
To leave a thousand-fold more bitter than
'Tis sweet at first to acquire,--after this process,
To give her the avaunt! it is a pity
Would move a monster.

Not for that reason either: here's the thing which hurts:
as her Highness has lived so long with her, and she
is such a good lady that nobody ever
had a bad word to say of her; I swear,
she never did any wrong: oh, now, having been
Queen for so many years,
still growing in majesty and dignity, leaving which
is a thousand times more bitter than the
sweetness of getting it–to send her away
after all that! It's so pitiful,
a monster would be moved by it.

Old Lady
Hearts of most hard temper
Melt and lament for her.

The hardest hearts
melt and weep for her.

ANNE
O, God's will! much better
She ne'er had known pomp: though't be temporal,
Yet, if that quarrel, fortune, do divorce
It from the bearer, 'tis a sufferance panging
As soul and body's severing.

Oh, God's will! It would be much better
if she had never had a position: although it is earthly,
if the blows of Fortune take it away
from one who has it feels as bad
as the separation of the soul and the body.

Old Lady
Alas, poor lady!
She's a stranger now again.

Alas, poor lady!
She is now a foreigner again.

ANNE
So much the more
Must pity drop upon her. Verily,
I swear, 'tis better to be lowly born,
And range with humble livers in content,
Than to be perk'd up in a glistering grief,
And wear a golden sorrow.

All the more reason
to give her pity. I swear
truly, it's better to be born low
and live happily and humbly
than to be decked out with glistening grief,
and wear a golden sorrow.

Old Lady
Our content
Is our best having.

Our happiness
is the greatest thing we have.

ANNE
By my troth and maidenhead,
I would not be a queen.

I swear on my maidenhood,
I don't want to be a queen.

Old Lady
Beshrew me, I would,
And venture maidenhead for't; and so would you,

For all this spice of your hypocrisy:
You, that have so fair parts of woman on you,
Have too a woman's heart; which ever yet
Affected eminence, wealth, sovereignty;
Which, to say sooth, are blessings; and which gifts,
Saving your mincing, the capacity
Of your soft cheveril conscience would receive,
If you might please to stretch it.

Believe me, I would,
and I would give my maidenhood for it; and so would you,
for all this hypocrisy you're showing:
with all your beauty and fine womanly qualities,
you also have a woman's heart; which has always
wanted power, wealth and rule;
which, to tell the truth, are blessings; and such gifts,
with all respect to your affectation, it would be within
the capability of your flexible conscience to accept,
if you were prepared to stretch the point.

ANNE
Nay, good troth.

No, I swear.

Old Lady
Yes, troth, and troth; you would not be a queen?

Yes, you swear, and swear; you don't want to be a queen?

ANNE
No, not for all the riches under heaven.

No, not for all the riches on earth.

Old Lady
'Tis strange: a three-pence bow'd would hire me,
Old as I am, to queen it: but, I pray you,
What think you of a duchess? have you limbs
To bear that load of title?

That's strange: a threepenny madam would hire me,
old as I am, to be a queen: but, may I ask,
what do you think of being a duchess? Are your limbs
strong enough to bear the load of that title?

ANNE
No, in truth.

I swear they are not.

Old Lady
Then you are weakly made: pluck off a little;
I would not be a young count in your way,
For more than blushing comes to: if your back
Cannot vouchsafe this burthen,'tis too weak
Ever to get a boy.

Then you are poorly made: calm down a little;
I wouldn't want to be a young count in your way,
for more than the price of a blush: if your back
won't accept this burden, you are too weak
to ever give birth to a boy.

ANNE
How you do talk!
I swear again, I would not be a queen
For all the world.

What things you say!
I swear again, I would not be a queen
for all the world.

Old Lady
In faith, for little England
You'ld venture an emballing: I myself
Would for Carnarvonshire, although there long'd
No more to the crown but that. Lo, who comes here?

I swear you would risk a coronation
for the sake of little England: I myself
would do it for Caernarfonshire, even if
that was all the Crown owned. Hello, who's this?

Enter Chamberlain

Chamberlain
Good morrow, ladies. What were't worth to know
The secret of your conference?

Good day, ladies. What would I have to pay to know
the secrets you're talking about?

ANNE
My good lord,
Not your demand; it values not your asking:
Our mistress' sorrows we were pitying.

My good lord,
not even your question; it's not worth you asking:
we were pitying the sorrows of our mistress.

Chamberlain
It was a gentle business, and becoming
The action of good women: there is hope
All will be well.

That is a kind business, and suited
to the action of good women: there is hope
that all will be well.

ANNE
Now, I pray God, amen!

I pray to God it may be so!

Chamberlain
You bear a gentle mind, and heavenly blessings
Follow such creatures. That you may, fair lady,
Perceive I speak sincerely, and high note's
Ta'en of your many virtues, the king's majesty
Commends his good opinion of you, and
Does purpose honour to you no less flowing
Than Marchioness of Pembroke: to which title
A thousand pound a year, annual support,
Out of his grace he adds.

You have a gentle mind, and heavenly blessings
come to such creatures. So that you, fair Lady,
may see that I speak sincerely, and that your many virtues
have been noticed by the highest, his Majesty the King
asks me to convey his good opinion of you, and
intends to honour you with no lesser title than
Marchioness of Pembroke: and from his kindness
he adds to the title a pension of a thousand pounds a year.

ANNE
I do not know

What kind of my obedience I should tender;
More than my all is nothing: nor my prayers
Are not words duly hallow'd, nor my wishes
More worth than empty vanities; yet prayers and wishes
Are all I can return. Beseech your lordship,
Vouchsafe to speak my thanks and my obedience,
As from a blushing handmaid, to his highness;
Whose health and royalty I pray for.

I do not know
how I should reply to this; everything I have is not enough: and my prayers
are not holy enough, and my wishes
are not worth more than empty trinkets; but prayers and wishes
are all I can give in return. I beg your Lordship,
be so kind as to give my thanks and my obedience,
as from a blushing handmaiden, to his Highness;
I pray for his health and his position.

Chamberlain
Lady,
I shall not fail to approve the fair conceit
The king hath of you.
Aside
I have perused her well;
Beauty and honour in her are so mingled
That they have caught the king: and who knows yet
But from this lady may proceed a gem
To lighten all this isle? I'll to the king,
And say I spoke with you.

Lady,
I won't fail to confirm the good opinion
the King has of you.
[Aside]
I have examined her well;
duty and honour are so mixed in her
that they have attracted the King: and who can tell
that this lady might not produce a gem
to brighten this whole island?

I'll go to the King,
and say I spoke with you.

Exit Chamberlain

ANNE

84

My honour'd lord.

My honoured Lord.

Old Lady
Why, this it is; see, see!
I have been begging sixteen years in court,
Am yet a courtier beggarly, nor could
Come pat betwixt too early and too late
For any suit of pounds; and you, O fate!
A very fresh-fish here--fie, fie, fie upon
This compell'd fortune!--have your mouth fill'd up
Before you open it.

Why this is it, see, see!
I have been begging in court for sixteen years,
and I'm still a begging courtier, and there's
nowhere at all that I could ever
get any sort of pension; and you, oh Fate!
An absolute greenhorn here–damnation to this
Fortune!–are given an absolute fortune
before you've even asked for it.

ANNE
This is strange to me.

This is strange to me.

Old Lady
How tastes it? is it bitter? forty pence, no.
There was a lady once, 'tis an old story,
That would not be a queen, that would she not,
For all the mud in Egypt: have you heard it?

How does it taste? Is it bitter? I'll bet forty pence it's not.
There was a lady once, it's an old story,
who said she wouldn't be Queen, that she wouldn't
for all the mud in Egypt: have you heard it?

ANNE
Come, you are pleasant.

Come, you are joking.

Old Lady
With your theme, I could

O'ermount the lark. The Marchioness of Pembroke!
A thousand pounds a year for pure respect!
No other obligation! By my life,
That promises moe thousands: honour's train
Is longer than his foreskirt. By this time
I know your back will bear a duchess: say,
Are you not stronger than you were?

If I had your reason to, I could
sing louder than the lark. The Marchioness of Pembroke!
A thousand pounds a year for nothing!
No job to do! I swear,
that promises more thousands: honour increases
as time goes on. I think this shows
that you could bear the title of Duchess: tell me,
aren't you stronger than you were before?

ANNE
Good lady,
Make yourself mirth with your particular fancy,
And leave me out on't. Would I had no being,
If this salute my blood a jot: it faints me,
To think what follows.
The queen is comfortless, and we forgetful
In our long absence: pray, do not deliver
What here you've heard to her.

Good lady,
amuse yourself with your strange fantasies,
and leave me out of it. I would wish myself dead
if this gave me any pleasure: it makes me faint,
to think of what will follow.
The Queen has no one to comfort her, and we are being forgetful
by being absent for so long: please, do not tell her
what you have heard here.

Old Lady
What do you think me?

Who do you think I am?

Exeunt

SCENE IV. A hall in Black-Friars.

Trumpets, sennet, and cornets. Enter two Vergers, with short silver wands; next them, two Scribes, in the habit of doctors; after them, CANTERBURY alone; after him, LINCOLN, Ely, Rochester, and Saint Asaph; next them, with some small distance, follows a Gentleman bearing the purse, with the great seal, and a cardinal's hat; then two Priests, bearing each a silver cross; then a Gentleman-usher bare-headed, accompanied with a Sergeant-at-arms bearing a silver mace; then two Gentlemen bearing two great silver pillars; after them, side by side, CARDINAL WOLSEY and CARDINAL CAMPEIUS; two Noblemen with the sword and mace. KING HENRY VIII takes place under the cloth of state; CARDINAL WOLSEY and CARDINAL CAMPEIUS sit under him as judges. QUEEN KATHARINE takes place some distance from KING HENRY VIII. The Bishops place themselves on each side the court, in manner of a consistory; below them, the Scribes. The Lords sit next the Bishops. The rest of the Attendants stand in convenient order about the stage.

CARDINAL WOLSEY
Whilst our commission from Rome is read,
Let silence be commanded.

Let there be silence
while our orders from Rome are read.

KING HENRY VIII
What's the need?
It hath already publicly been read,
And on all sides the authority allow'd;
You may, then, spare that time.

What need is there?
They have already been read out publicly,
and everybody has agreed to their authority;
you can save that trouble.

CARDINAL WOLSEY
Be't so. Proceed.

So be it. Carry on.

Scribe
Say, Henry King of England, come into the court.

Henry King of England, come into the court.

Crier
Henry King of England, & c.

Henry King of England!

KING HENRY VIII
Here.

I am here.

Scribe
Say, Katharine Queen of England, come into the court.

Katherine, Queen of England, come in to the court!

Crier
Katharine Queen of England, & c.

Katherine Queen of England!

QUEEN KATHARINE makes no answer, rises out of her chair, goes about the court, comes to KING HENRY VIII, and kneels at his feet; then speaks

QUEEN KATHARINE
Sir, I desire you do me right and justice;
And to bestow your pity on me: for
I am a most poor woman, and a stranger,
Born out of your dominions; having here
No judge indifferent, nor no more assurance
Of equal friendship and proceeding. Alas, sir,
In what have I offended you? what cause
Hath my behavior given to your displeasure,
That thus you should proceed to put me off,
And take your good grace from me? Heaven witness,
I have been to you a true and humble wife,
At all times to your will conformable;
Ever in fear to kindle your dislike,
Yea, subject to your countenance, glad or sorry
As I saw it inclined: when was the hour
I ever contradicted your desire,
Or made it not mine too? Or which of your friends
Have I not strove to love, although I knew
He were mine enemy? what friend of mine
That had to him derived your anger, did I
Continue in my liking? nay, gave notice

He was from thence discharged. Sir, call to mind
That I have been your wife, in this obedience,
Upward of twenty years, and have been blest
With many children by you: if, in the course
And process of this time, you can report,
And prove it too, against mine honour aught,
My bond to wedlock, or my love and duty,
Against your sacred person, in God's name,
Turn me away; and let the foul'st contempt
Shut door upon me, and so give me up
To the sharp'st kind of justice. Please you sir,
The king, your father, was reputed for
A prince most prudent, of an excellent
And unmatch'd wit and judgment: Ferdinand,
My father, king of Spain, was reckon'd one
The wisest prince that there had reign'd by many
A year before: it is not to be question'd
That they had gather'd a wise council to them
Of every realm, that did debate this business,
Who deem'd our marriage lawful: wherefore I humbly
Beseech you, sir, to spare me, till I may
Be by my friends in Spain advised; whose counsel
I will implore: if not, i' the name of God,
Your pleasure be fulfill'd!

Sir, I ask you to give me my rights and justice, and to give me your pity; for
I am a very poor woman, and a foreigner,
born outside your kingdom: I do not have
an impartial judge here, nor any assurance
that I will be treated equally or with justice. Alas, Sir,
how have I offended you? What reason
has my behaviour given you to be displeased,
so that you take these steps to discard me
and take away your good grace from me? As heaven is my witness,
I have been a faithful and obedient wife to you,
always obeying your will,
always afraid to attract your dislike,
always following your moods, happy or sad
as I saw you. When did I ever
go against your wishes
or refuse to imitate you? Which of your friends
have I not tried to love, even if I knew
he was my enemy? What friend of mine
did I carry on liking if he had
annoyed you? When did I fail
to send him away? Sir, remember

that I have been your obedient wife
for more than twenty years, and have been blessed
with many children by you. If over
this period you can point to,
with proof, anything against my honour,
my marriage vows, or my love and duty
to your holy person; then in God's name
turn me away, and let the foulest contempt
close the door upon me, and abandon me
to the harshest kind of justice. If you please, sir,
your father the King had a reputation as being
a very prudent prince, with excellent,
matchless intelligence and judgement: Ferdinand
my father, King of Spain, was thought to be
the wisest prince who had ruled there
for many years. It is beyond doubt
that they gathered a wise council around them
from every country, and they debated this business,
and agreed our marriage was lawful: and so I humbly
beg you sir to spare me until I may
be advised by my friends in Spain, whose advice
I will ask for. If not, may you to what you wish
in the name of God.

CARDINAL WOLSEY
You have here, lady,
And of your choice, these reverend fathers; men
Of singular integrity and learning,
Yea, the elect o' the land, who are assembled
To plead your cause: it shall be therefore bootless
That longer you desire the court; as well
For your own quiet, as to rectify
What is unsettled in the king.

You have here, Lady,
these respected priests of your choice; men
of unique integrity and learning,
the greatest in the land, who have gathered
to plead your cause: so it's pointless
to ask the court for more time; as much
for your own peace of mind, as to
settle the king's.

CARDINAL CAMPEIUS
His grace
Hath spoken well and justly: therefore, madam,

It's fit this royal session do proceed;
And that, without delay, their arguments
Be now produced and heard.

His Grace
has spoken well and fairly: therefore, madam,
it's right that this royal court should proceed;
and that, without delay, their arguments
should now be produced and heard.

QUEEN KATHARINE
Lord cardinal,
To you I speak.

Lord Cardinal,
I am addressing you.

CARDINAL WOLSEY
Your pleasure, madam?

What is it you wish, madam?

QUEEN KATHARINE
Sir,
I am about to weep; but, thinking that
We are a queen, or long have dream'd so, certain
The daughter of a king, my drops of tears
I'll turn to sparks of fire.

Sir,
I am about to weep; but, thinking that
I am a Queen, or I have certainly dreamt I am for a long time,
and certainly I am the daughter of the King, my teardrops
will turn into sparks of fire.

CARDINAL WOLSEY
Be patient yet.

Remain calm.

QUEEN KATHARINE
I will, when you are humble; nay, before,
Or God will punish me. I do believe,
Induced by potent circumstances, that
You are mine enemy, and make my challenge
You shall not be my judge: for it is you

Have blown this coal betwixt my lord and me;
Which God's dew quench! Therefore I say again,
I utterly abhor, yea, from my soul
Refuse you for my judge; whom, yet once more,
I hold my most malicious foe, and think not
At all a friend to truth.

I shall be, when you are humble; in fact before that,
or God will punish me. I believe,
due to strong evidence, that
you are my enemy, and I ask
that you should not be my judge: it is you
who has stirred up this storm between my lord and me;
may God's sweetness calm it! And so I say again,
I utterly refuse, from the depths of my soul,
to have you as my judge; someone whom, I say again,
I think is my most vicious enemy, and I do not think
a truthful one.

CARDINAL WOLSEY
I do profess
You speak not like yourself; who ever yet
Have stood to charity, and display'd the effects
Of disposition gentle, and of wisdom
O'ertopping woman's power. Madam, you do me wrong:
I have no spleen against you; nor injustice
For you or any: how far I have proceeded,
Or how far further shall, is warranted
By a commission from the consistory,
Yea, the whole consistory of Rome. You charge me
That I have blown this coal: I do deny it:
The king is present: if it be known to him
That I gainsay my deed, how may he wound,
And worthily, my falsehood! yea, as much
As you have done my truth. If he know
That I am free of your report, he knows
I am not of your wrong. Therefore in him
It lies to cure me: and the cure is, to
Remove these thoughts from you: the which before
His highness shall speak in, I do beseech
You, gracious madam, to unthink your speaking
And to say so no more.

I swear
that you are not yourself; you have always
been kind and shown the effects

of a gentle nature, and of wisdom
greater than most women. Madam, you wrong me:
I have no anger against you, and will be unjust
to nobody: what I have done,
and what I shall do in future, is ordered
by the college of cardinals,
the whole college of Rome. You charge me
with fanning the flames: I deny it;
the King is here; if he knows
that I have done it and now deny it, he can
expose my lies, and rightly so, as much
as you have exposed my truth. If he knows
that I am innocent of what you say, he knows
I am not here to do you harm. So it is
down to him to acquit me, and the way to do that
is to stop you thinking this way: and so before
his Highness speaks, I beg you,
gracious madam, to stop thinking this way
and to stop saying these things.

QUEEN KATHARINE
My lord, my lord,
I am a simple woman, much too weak
To oppose your cunning. You're meek and
humble-mouth'd;
You sign your place and calling, in full seeming,
With meekness and humility; but your heart
Is cramm'd with arrogancy, spleen, and pride.
You have, by fortune and his highness' favours,
Gone slightly o'er low steps and now are mounted
Where powers are your retainers, and your words,
Domestics to you, serve your will as't please
Yourself pronounce their office. I must tell you,
You tender more your person's honour than
Your high profession spiritual: that again
I do refuse you for my judge; and here,
Before you all, appeal unto the pope,
To bring my whole cause 'fore his holiness,
And to be judged by him.

My lord, my lord,
I am a simple woman, much too weak
to fight your cunning. You are meek and speak humbly;
you show your position and your calling, it seems,
with meekness and humility; but your heart
is crammed with arrogance, anger and pride.

You have, by luck and the goodwill of his Highness,
leapt easily over the low rungs and have now climbed
up where great men do your bidding, and your words,
servants to you, make them do whatever
you order. I must tell you,
your personal position is more important to you than
your great spiritual profession: that once again
I refuse to let you be my judge; and here,
in front of you all, I appeal to the Pope,
I ask for my whole case to be brought before his holiness,
and to be judged by him.

She curtsies to KING HENRY VIII, and offers to depart

CARDINAL CAMPEIUS
The queen is obstinate,
Stubborn to justice, apt to accuse it, and
Disdainful to be tried by't: 'tis not well.
She's going away.

The Queen is obstinate,
opposed to justice, inclined to accuse it
and unwilling to be tried by it: this is not good.
She's going away.

KING HENRY VIII
Call her again.

Call her back.

Crier
Katharine Queen of England, come into the court.

Katherine Queen of England, come into the court.

GRIFFITH
Madam, you are call'd back.

Madam, you have been called back.

QUEEN KATHARINE
What need you note it? pray you, keep your way:
When you are call'd, return. Now, the Lord help,
They vex me past my patience! Pray you, pass on:
I will not tarry; no, nor ever more

Upon this business my appearance make
In any of their courts.

Why do you need to say it? Please, keep going:
when you are called, come back. Now, Lord help me,
they are vexing me beyond endurance! Please, move on:
I will not stay; no, nor will I ever
appear again in any of their courts
on this business.

Exeunt QUEEN KATHARINE and her Attendants

KING HENRY VIII
Go thy ways, Kate:
That man i' the world who shall report he has
A better wife, let him in nought be trusted,
For speaking false in that: thou art, alone,
If thy rare qualities, sweet gentleness,
Thy meekness saint-like, wife-like government,
Obeying in commanding, and thy parts
Sovereign and pious else, could speak thee out,
The queen of earthly queens: she's noble born;
And, like her true nobility, she has
Carried herself towards me.

Go where you like, Kate:
if any man in the world says he has
a better wife, don't trust him,
he's lying: no one compares to you,
if your unique qualities, sweet gentleness,
your saintly meekness, your wifely rule,
your obedience and all your other
royal and holy qualities could speak out loud for you
they would name you the Queen of all queens on earth:
she is nobly born; and she has behaved towards me
with true nobility.

CARDINAL WOLSEY
Most gracious sir,
In humblest manner I require your highness,
That it shall please you to declare, in hearing
Of all these ears,--for where I am robb'd and bound,
There must I be unloosed, although not there
At once and fully satisfied,--whether ever I
Did broach this business to your highness; or
Laid any scruple in your way, which might

Induce you to the question on't? or ever
Have to you, but with thanks to God for such
A royal lady, spake one the least word that might
Be to the prejudice of her present state,
Or touch of her good person?

Most gracious Sir,
I must ask your Highness in the most humble way
 that you should declare for everyone
to hear–for I must be cleared
of these accusations, they cannot
be left for a moment–whether I ever
spoke of this business to your Highness; or
gave you any reason to doubt, which might
have made you question it? Or have you
ever said anything about the Royal lady,
apart from giving your thanks to God for her,
which might in any way cast doubt upon her character
or place her in a difficult position?

KING HENRY VIII
My lord cardinal,
I do excuse you; yea, upon mine honour,
I free you from't. You are not to be taught
That you have many enemies, that know not
Why they are so, but, like to village-curs,
Bark when their fellows do: by some of these
The queen is put in anger. You're excused:
But will you be more justified? You ever
Have wish'd the sleeping of this business; never desired
It to be stirr'd; but oft have hinder'd, oft,
The passages made toward it: on my honour,
I speak my good lord cardinal to this point,
And thus far clear him. Now, what moved me to't,
I will be bold with time and your attention:
Then mark the inducement. Thus it came; give heed to't:
My conscience first received a tenderness,
Scruple, and prick, on certain speeches utter'd
By the Bishop of Bayonne, then French ambassador;
Who had been hither sent on the debating
A marriage 'twixt the Duke of Orleans and
Our daughter Mary: i' the progress of this business,
Ere a determinate resolution, he,
I mean the bishop, did require a respite;
Wherein he might the king his lord advertise
Whether our daughter were legitimate,

Respecting this our marriage with the dowager,
Sometimes our brother's wife. This respite shook
The bosom of my conscience, enter'd me,
Yea, with a splitting power, and made to tremble
The region of my breast; which forced such way,
That many mazed considerings did throng
And press'd in with this caution. First, methought
I stood not in the smile of heaven; who had
Commanded nature, that my lady's womb,
If it conceived a male child by me, should
Do no more offices of life to't than
The grave does to the dead; for her male issue
Or died where they were made, or shortly after
This world had air'd them: hence I took a thought,
This was a judgment on me; that my kingdom,
Well worthy the best heir o' the world, should not
Be gladded in't by me: then follows, that
I weigh'd the danger which my realms stood in
By this my issue's fail; and that gave to me
Many a groaning throe. Thus hulling in
The wild sea of my conscience, I did steer
Toward this remedy, whereupon we are
Now present here together: that's to say,
I meant to rectify my conscience,--which
I then did feel full sick, and yet not well,--
By all the reverend fathers of the land
And doctors learn'd: first I began in private
With you, my Lord of Lincoln; you remember
How under my oppression I did reek,
When I first moved you.

My Lord Cardinal,
I exonerate you; I excuse you
upon my honour; you do not have to be told
that you have many enemies who do not know
why they hate you, but like village dogs
bark when their friends do. The Queen has been
made angry by people like that; you are excused:
but shall I say more in your defence? You always
wanted this business to be left alone, you never
wanted it to be stirred up, you have often blocked me
when I have try to instigate proceedings; I swear,
I can speak for my good lord cardinal on this point,
and so clear him. As for what motivated me,
I will take up some time and your attention:
take note of my reasons, this is what happened, listen:

my conscience was first pricked
with doubt because of certain speeches made
by the Bishop of Bayonne, then French ambassador,
who had been sent here to debate the issue
of a marriage between the Duke of Orleans and
my daughter Mary: as this business went on,
before they reached a decision, he
—I mean the Bishop—wanted a pause,
so that he could inform his lord the king
whether my daughter was legitimate
as I was married to the woman
who was once my brother's wife. This request shook
the heart of my conscience, got into my mind,
it transfixed me, and made me tremble
in my heart, and gave birth to
such perplexed thoughts that it created
these worries. Firstly, I thought
that I was out of favour with God, who had
commanded nature that if my lady conceived
a male child by me then her womb would no more
give it life than a grave gives life to the dead:
her male children either died as they were born or
shortly afterwards. So I thought that
this was a judgement on me, that my kingdom
—which well deserves the best heir in the world—would not
be made happy through me. In consequence
I thought of the danger my kingdom was in
if I did not produce an heir, and that gave me
many great pains: so drifting across
the wild sea of my conscience, I steered towards
this solution, which is why we are
all here today: I mean to say,
I wanted to pacify my conscience,
which was then making me feel quite sick,
and I couldn't be cured by all the holy fathers of the land
and all the learned doctors. I first spoke privately
to you, my Lord of Lincoln; you remember
how I sweated under the weight of my distress
when I first confessed it to you.

LINCOLN
Very well, my liege.

I remember very well, my lord.

KING HENRY VIII

I have spoke long: be pleased yourself to say
How far you satisfied me.

I have spoken for a long time; please say yourself
how far you managed to reassure me.

LINCOLN
So please your highness,
The question did at first so stagger me,
Bearing a state of mighty moment in't
And consequence of dread, that I committed
The daring'st counsel which I had to doubt;
And did entreat your highness to this course
Which you are running here.

If it pleases your Highness,
the question at first was so staggering,
being so important for the country
and with the risk of such dreadful consequences,
that I did not trust the most daring solution
which occurred to me, and I told your Highness to follow
the course which you are now taking.

KING HENRY VIII
I then moved you,
My Lord of Canterbury; and got your leave
To make this present summons: unsolicited
I left no reverend person in this court;
But by particular consent proceeded
Under your hands and seals: therefore, go on:
For no dislike i' the world against the person
Of the good queen, but the sharp thorny points
Of my alleged reasons, drive this forward:
Prove but our marriage lawful, by my life
And kingly dignity, we are contented
To wear our mortal state to come with her,
Katharine our queen, before the primest creature
That's paragon'd o' the world.

I then asked you,
my Lord of Canterbury; and I got your permission
to begin these current proceedings: I did not
fail to ask any holy person in this Court;
I moved forward with your specific agreement,
signed and sealed: so, proceed:
there is no dislike in any way of

the good Queen motivating this,
it's only the sharp pricks of the
reasons I have put forward:
if you can prove that our marriage is lawful, I swear on my life
and my dignity as a king, I shall be happy
to spend the rest of my life with her,
Katherine my Queen, ahead of anyone
who is put forward as the finest creature in the world.

CARDINAL CAMPEIUS
So please your highness,
The queen being absent, 'tis a needful fitness
That we adjourn this court till further day:
Meanwhile must be an earnest motion
Made to the queen, to call back her appeal
She intends unto his holiness.

If it pleases your Highness,
with the Queen being absent, it is necessary
for us to adjourn this court until another day:
in the meantime earnest efforts must be made
to persuade the Queen not to make the appeal
to the Pope which she intends.

KING HENRY VIII
[Aside] I may perceive
These cardinals trifle with me: I abhor
This dilatory sloth and tricks of Rome.
My learn'd and well-beloved servant, Cranmer,
Prithee, return: with thy approach, I know,
My comfort comes along. Break up the court:
I say, set on.

I can see
that these cardinals are trifling with me: I hate
this lazy slowness and tricks of Rome.
My learned and much loved servant, Cranmer,
I pray for your return: I know that when you come
you will help me. Break up the court:
I say, move along.

Exeunt in manner as they entered

Act III

SCENE I. London. QUEEN KATHARINE's apartments.

Enter QUEEN KATHARINE and her Women, as at work

QUEEN KATHARINE
Take thy lute, wench: my soul grows sad with troubles;
Sing, and disperse 'em, if thou canst: leave working.

Pick up your lute, girl: all these troubles have made me sad;
sing, and blow them away, if you can: leave your work.

SONG
Orpheus with his lute made trees,
And the mountain tops that freeze,
Bow themselves when he did sing:
To his music plants and flowers
Ever sprung; as sun and showers
There had made a lasting spring.
Every thing that heard him play,
Even the billows of the sea,
Hung their heads, and then lay by.
In sweet music is such art,
Killing care and grief of heart
Fall asleep, or hearing, die.

With his lute Orpheus made the trees,
and the frozen mountaintops,
bow down to him when he sang:
plants and flowers always sprung up
at his music; as if the sun and showers
had made an eternal spring there.
Everything that heard him play,
even the waves of the sea,
hung their heads, and then lay around him.
There is such art in sweet music
that it can kill troubles and the sadness of the heart
falls asleep or, hearing, dies.

Enter a Gentleman

QUEEN KATHARINE
How now!

Hello there!

Gentleman
An't please your grace, the two great cardinals
Wait in the presence.

*If you please, your grace, the two great cardinals
are waiting in your meeting room.*

QUEEN KATHARINE
Would they speak with me?

Do they want to speak with me?

Gentleman
They will'd me say so, madam.

They told me to tell you so, madam.

QUEEN KATHARINE
Pray their graces
To come near.

*Ask their graces
to come in.*

Exit Gentleman
What can be their business
With me, a poor weak woman, fall'n from favour?
I do not like their coming. Now I think on't,
They should be good men; their affairs as righteous:
But all hoods make not monks.

*What business can they have
with me, a poor weak woman, out-of-favour?
I don't like their being here. Now I think about it,
they should be good men; their business should be holy:
but it takes more than a hood to make a monk.*

Enter CARDINAL WOLSEY and CARDINAL CAMPEIUS

CARDINAL WOLSEY
Peace to your highness!

Peace be with your Highness!

QUEEN KATHARINE
Your graces find me here part of a housewife,
I would be all, against the worst may happen.
What are your pleasures with me, reverend lords?

Your graces find me here acting the part of a housewife,
I wish I really was one, if the worst should happen.
What do you want with me, reverend lords?

CARDINAL WOLSEY
May it please you noble madam, to withdraw
Into your private chamber, we shall give you
The full cause of our coming.

If you would like to withdraw into your
private chamber, noble madam, we shall
give you a full explanation of why we are here.

QUEEN KATHARINE
Speak it here:
There's nothing I have done yet, o' my conscience,
Deserves a corner: would all other women
Could speak this with as free a soul as I do!
My lords, I care not, so much I am happy
Above a number, if my actions
Were tried by every tongue, every eye saw 'em,
Envy and base opinion set against 'em,
I know my life so even. If your business
Seek me out, and that way I am wife in,
Out with it boldly: truth loves open dealing.

Say it here:
I can swear that I have done nothing that
needs hiding: if only all other women
could say this with as clear a conscience as I do!
My lords, I do not care (I am so much better
than many others) if my actions
were judged by every tongue, if every eye saw them,
if malice and low opinions were set on them,
I know my life is blameless. If your business
concerns me and my place as a wife,
speak out boldly: truth loves openness.

CARDINAL WOLSEY
Tanta est erga te mentis integritas, regina

serenissima,--

Tanta est erga te mentis integritas, regina
serenissima,--

QUEEN KATHARINE
O, good my lord, no Latin;
I am not such a truant since my coming,
As not to know the language I have lived in:
A strange tongue makes my cause more strange,
suspicious;
Pray, speak in English: here are some will thank you,
If you speak truth, for their poor mistress' sake;
Believe me, she has had much wrong: lord cardinal,
The willing'st sin I ever yet committed
May be absolved in English.

Oh, my good lord, no Latin;
I have not been such a bad pupil since I came here
that I don't know the language of the place I have lived in;
a foreign tongue makes the business looks strange and suspicious;
please, speak in English: there are some here who will thank you
if you speak the truth, for the sake of her poor mistress;
believe me, she has been very wronged: lord cardinal,
the most deliberate sin I have ever committed
may be forgiven in English.

CARDINAL WOLSEY
Noble lady,
I am sorry my integrity should breed,
And service to his majesty and you,
So deep suspicion, where all faith was meant.
We come not by the way of accusation,
To taint that honour every good tongue blesses,
Nor to betray you any way to sorrow,
You have too much, good lady; but to know
How you stand minded in the weighty difference
Between the king and you; and to deliver,
Like free and honest men, our just opinions
And comforts to your cause.

Noble lady,
I'm sorry that my integrity should cause
(and my service to his Majesty and to you)
such deep suspicion, where I am acting faithfully.
We have not come to accuse you,

to insult the honour that every good person's tongue praises,
nor to bring you any sorrow,
you have too much already, good lady; but to ask
what your thoughts are about the great disagreements
between the king and you; and to offer,
like guiltless and honest men, our true opinions
and help to you.

CARDINAL CAMPEIUS
Most honour'd madam,
My Lord of York, out of his noble nature,
Zeal and obedience he still bore your grace,
Forgetting, like a good man your late censure
Both of his truth and him, which was too far,
Offers, as I do, in a sign of peace,
His service and his counsel.

Most honoured madam,
my Lord of York, because of his noble nature,
the passion and obedience he still has for your grace,
is prepared like a good man to forget your recent criticism
of both his honesty and him, which was too great,
offers you, as I do, as a token of peace,
his service and his advice.

QUEEN KATHARINE
[Aside] To betray me.--
My lords, I thank you both for your good wills;
Ye speak like honest men; pray God, ye prove so!
But how to make ye suddenly an answer,
In such a point of weight, so near mine honour,--
More near my life, I fear,--with my weak wit,
And to such men of gravity and learning,
In truth, I know not. I was set at work
Among my maids: full little, God knows, looking
Either for such men or such business.
For her sake that I have been,--for I feel
The last fit of my greatness,--good your graces,
Let me have time and counsel for my cause:
Alas, I am a woman, friendless, hopeless!

To betray me–
my Lords, I thank you both for your goodwill;
you speak like honest men; I pray to God that you will prove to be!
But how I can give you a quick answer,
on such an important matter, which affects my honour so much–

and even more affects my life, I fear–with my poor intelligence,
to men of such dignity and learning,
I really don't know. I was sitting working
amongst my maids: God knows I was not expecting
to see such men or be faced with such matters;
for the sake of the woman I used to be (for I can feel
that my greatness has almost gone) may your good graces
allow me to have time to think and take advice on the matter:
alas, I am a friendless and hopeless woman.

CARDINAL WOLSEY
Madam, you wrong the king's love with these fears:
Your hopes and friends are infinite.

Madam, you insult the King's love by fearing this:
you have an infinite number of friends and great hope.

QUEEN KATHARINE
In England
But little for my profit: can you think, lords,
That any Englishman dare give me counsel?
Or be a known friend, 'gainst his highness' pleasure,
Though he be grown so desperate to be honest,
And live a subject? Nay, forsooth, my friends,
They that must weigh out my afflictions,
They that my trust must grow to, live not here:
They are, as all my other comforts, far hence
In mine own country, lords.

None to
offer me much hope in England: can you think, lords,
of any Englishman who would dare to give me advice?
Or to be known as my friend, against the wishes of his Highness,
however reckless he was to say what he thought,
and still live as a subject? No, in truth, my friends,
those who can compensate for my suffering,
the ones I must give my trust to, do not live here:
they are, as is everything else which can comfort me, far away
in my own country, my lords.

CARDINAL CAMPEIUS
I would your grace
Would leave your griefs, and take my counsel.

I wish your Grace
would abandon your sorrow, and take my advice.

QUEEN KATHARINE
How, sir?

What is it, sir?

CARDINAL CAMPEIUS
Put your main cause into the king's protection;
He's loving and most gracious: 'twill be much
Both for your honour better and your cause;
For if the trial of the law o'ertake ye,
You'll part away disgraced.

Put yourself under the King's protection;
he's loving and most gracious: it will be much
better for both your honour and your cause;
if you have to go to trial
you will leave disgraced.

CARDINAL WOLSEY
He tells you rightly.

He's telling the truth.

QUEEN KATHARINE
Ye tell me what ye wish for both,--my ruin:
Is this your Christian counsel? out upon ye!
Heaven is above all yet; there sits a judge
That no king can corrupt.

You're telling me what you both want—my ruin:
is this your Christian advice? Get out!
Heaven is still sitting over all of us; there is a judge there
that cannot be corrupted by any king.

CARDINAL CAMPEIUS
Your rage mistakes us.

You have misunderstood us in your anger.

QUEEN KATHARINE
The more shame for ye: holy men I thought ye,
Upon my soul, two reverend cardinal virtues;
But cardinal sins and hollow hearts I fear ye:
Mend 'em, for shame, my lords. Is this your comfort?
The cordial that ye bring a wretched lady,

A woman lost among ye, laugh'd at, scorn'd?
I will not wish ye half my miseries;
I have more charity: but say, I warn'd ye;
Take heed, for heaven's sake, take heed, lest at once
The burthen of my sorrows fall upon ye.

Shame on you: I thought you were holy men,
I swear, two holy good Cardinals;
but I fear you are great sinners with hollow hearts:
mend your ways, my lords, for shame. Is this your comfort?
The medicine that you bring for a wretched lady,
a woman lost amongst you, laughed at, scorned?
I would not wish you half my misery;
I am more charitable: but take note of my warning;
be careful, for heaven's sake, be careful, in case
the weight of my sorrows should suddenly fall upon you.

CARDINAL WOLSEY
Madam, this is a mere distraction;
You turn the good we offer into envy.

Madam, this is just madness;
you make our kind offers seem malicious.

QUEEN KATHARINE
Ye turn me into nothing: woe upon ye
And all such false professors! would you have me--
If you have any justice, any pity;
If ye be any thing but churchmen's habits--
Put my sick cause into his hands that hates me?
Alas, has banish'd me his bed already,
His love, too long ago! I am old, my lords,
And all the fellowship I hold now with him
Is only my obedience. What can happen
To me above this wretchedness? all your studies
Make me a curse like this.

You make me nothing: damn you
and all such false Christians! Do you want me–
if you have any justice, any pity;
if you're anything more than empty robes–
to place my wounded life into the hands of one who hates me?
Alas, I am already an exile from his bed,
and from his love, too long ago! I am old, my lords,
and the only business I have with him now I do
out of my obedience. What can happen

to me that's worse than this? Everything you do
brings me all this misery.

CARDINAL CAMPEIUS
Your fears are worse.

What you fear is worse than the reality of it.

QUEEN KATHARINE
Have I lived thus long--let me speak myself,
Since virtue finds no friends--a wife, a true one?
A woman, I dare say without vain-glory,
Never yet branded with suspicion?
Have I with all my full affections
Still met the king? loved him next heaven?
obey'd him?
Been, out of fondness, superstitious to him?
Almost forgot my prayers to content him?
And am I thus rewarded? 'tis not well, lords.
Bring me a constant woman to her husband,
One that ne'er dream'd a joy beyond his pleasure;
And to that woman, when she has done most,
Yet will I add an honour, a great patience.

Have I lived so long—let me speak for myself,
since goodness has no friends—as a wife, a true one?
The woman, I daresay without vanity,
never yet suspected of any wrongdoing?
Have I always given all my love
to the King? Loved him more than anything outside Heaven?
Obeyed him?
In my foolishness been extravagantly devoted to him?
Almost abandoned my prayers to make him happy?
And is this how I am rewarded? It is not good, lords.
Show me a woman who is loyal to her husband,
one who never sought for any happiness beyond his pleasure,
and when that woman has done all she can
I will still be ahead of her, due to my great patience.

CARDINAL WOLSEY
Madam, you wander from the good we aim at.

Madam, you are missing the point of the good we intend for you.

QUEEN KATHARINE
My lord, I dare not make myself so guilty,

To give up willingly that noble title
Your master wed me to: nothing but death
Shall e'er divorce my dignities.

My lord, I do not dare to make myself so guilty
that I would willingly give up that noble title
your master gave me when we married: nothing but death
will ever take away my honour.

CARDINAL WOLSEY
Pray, hear me.

Please, listen to me.

QUEEN KATHARINE
Would I had never trod this English earth,
Or felt the flatteries that grow upon it!
Ye have angels' faces, but heaven knows your hearts.
What will become of me now, wretched lady!
I am the most unhappy woman living.
Alas, poor wenches, where are now your fortunes!
Shipwreck'd upon a kingdom, where no pity,
No friend, no hope; no kindred weep for me;
Almost no grave allow'd me: like the lily,
That once was mistress of the field and flourish'd,
I'll hang my head and perish.

I wish I had never walked on this English earth,
or felt the flattery that grows on it!
You have the faces of angels, but heaven knows what's in your hearts.
What will happen to me now, wretched lady!
I am the unhappiest woman alive.
Alas, poor girls, now where are your fortunes!
Shipwrecked in the kingdom where there is no pity,
no friends, no hope; no family to weep for me;
I will almost be denied burial: I shall hang my head
and die, like a lily that at one time was the mistress of the field.

CARDINAL WOLSEY
If your grace
Could but be brought to know our ends are honest,
You'ld feel more comfort: why should we, good lady,
Upon what cause, wrong you? alas, our places,
The way of our profession is against it:
We are to cure such sorrows, not to sow 'em.
For goodness' sake, consider what you do;

How you may hurt yourself, ay, utterly
Grow from the king's acquaintance, by this carriage.
The hearts of princes kiss obedience,
So much they love it; but to stubborn spirits
They swell, and grow as terrible as storms.
I know you have a gentle, noble temper,
A soul as even as a calm: pray, think us
Those we profess, peace-makers, friends, and servants.

If your Grace
could only see that our purposes are honest,
you would be happier. Why should we, good lady,
and for what reason, harm you? Alas, our positions
and the obligations of our calling are against it;
we have to heal such sorrows, not cause them.
For goodness' sake think of what you do,
how you can damage yourself, completely
alienate the King by this behaviour.
The hearts of Princes kiss obedience,
they love it so much; but to people who are stubborn
they become like terrible storms.
I know you have a gentle and noble disposition,
and your soul is just as calm; please think that we are
what we say we are, peacemakers, friends and servants

CARDINAL CAMPEIUS
Madam, you'll find it so. You wrong your virtues
With these weak women's fears: a noble spirit,
As yours was put into you, ever casts
Such doubts, as false coin, from it. The king loves you;
Beware you lose it not: for us, if you please
To trust us in your business, we are ready
To use our utmost studies in your service.

Madam, you'll find this is true. You are insulting your goodness
with these weak womanish fears: a noble spirit,
such was the one you have, always pushes
these doubts away, like counterfeit money. The King loves you;
make sure you don't lose that love: as for us, if you
will trust us with your business, we are ready
to do our very best to serve you.

QUEEN KATHARINE
Do what ye will, my lords: and, pray, forgive me,
If I have used myself unmannerly;
You know I am a woman, lacking wit

To make a seemly answer to such persons.
Pray, do my service to his majesty:
He has my heart yet; and shall have my prayers
While I shall have my life. Come, reverend fathers,
Bestow your counsels on me: she now begs,
That little thought, when she set footing here,
She should have bought her dignities so dear.

Do what you want, my lords: and please forgive me
if I have shown a lack of manners;
you know I am a woman, without the intelligence
to make a proper answer to such people.
Please, give my compliments to his Majesty:
he still has my heart, and he shall have my prayers
as long as I have my life. Come, reverend fathers,
give me your advice: this woman is now begging,
who hardly thought, when she set foot in this land,
that she would pay such a high price for her titles.

Exeunt

SCENE II. Ante-chamber to KING HENRY VIII's apartment.

Enter NORFOLK, SUFFOLK, SURREY, and Chamberlain

NORFOLK
If you will now unite in your complaints,
And force them with a constancy, the cardinal
Cannot stand under them: if you omit
The offer of this time, I cannot promise
But that you shall sustain moe new disgraces,
With these you bear already.

If you will now be united in your complaints,
and insist on them with determination, the cardinal
cannot avoid them: if you miss
this chance, I can't guarantee
that you won't suffer more disgraces to add
to those you already have.

SURREY
I am joyful
To meet the least occasion that may give me
Remembrance of my father-in-law, the duke,
To be revenged on him.

I am happy
to take any opportunity I'm given
to take revenge in memory of
my father-in-law the Duke.

SUFFOLK
Which of the peers
Have uncontemn'd gone by him, or at least
Strangely neglected? when did he regard
The stamp of nobleness in any person
Out of himself?

Is there any peer
who has not suffered his contempt, or at least
been oddly ignored? When did he respect
nobility in any person
apart from himself?

Chamberlain
My lords, you speak your pleasures:
What he deserves of you and me I know;
What we can do to him, though now the time
Gives way to us, I much fear. If you cannot
Bar his access to the king, never attempt
Any thing on him; for he hath a witchcraft
Over the king in's tongue.

My lords, you say what you want:
I know what he deserves from us;
I am worried about what we can do to him,
even though we now have the opportunity. If you cannot
stop him talking to the King, do not try
anything against him; for his tongue
casts a spell over the King.

NORFOLK
O, fear him not;
His spell in that is out: the king hath found
Matter against him that for ever mars
The honey of his language. No, he's settled,
Not to come off, in his displeasure.

Oh, do not be afraid of him;
he has lost his magic in that: the King has discovered
things against him that have permanently removed
the power of his words. No, he's adamant
that he shall not escape his displeasure.

SURREY
Sir,
I should be glad to hear such news as this
Once every hour.

Sir,
I would be glad to hear news like this
every hour on the hour.

NORFOLK
Believe it, this is true:
In the divorce his contrary proceedings
Are all unfolded wherein he appears
As I would wish mine enemy.

Believe it, it's true:
the divorce has revealed his opposition
to the King and he now stands in as bad a light
as I would wish for my enemy.

SURREY
How came
His practises to light?

How did
his machinations come to light?

SUFFOLK
Most strangely.

Very strangely.

SURREY
O, how, how?

How, how?

SUFFOLK
The cardinal's letters to the pope miscarried,
And came to the eye o' the king: wherein was read,
How that the cardinal did entreat his holiness
To stay the judgment o' the divorce; for if
It did take place, 'I do,' quoth he, 'perceive
My king is tangled in affection to
A creature of the queen's, Lady Anne Bullen.'

The cardinal's letters to the Pope went astray,
and the King saw them: and he read in them
how the cardinal urged his Holiness
to delay the judgement of the divorce; for if
it takes place, 'I do,' he said, 'see
that my king has become entangled with
one of the Queen's servants, Lady Anne Bullen.'

SURREY
Has the king this?

And the King knows this?

SUFFOLK

Believe it.

Certainly.

SURREY
Will this work?

Will this have an effect?

Chamberlain
The king in this perceives him, how he coasts
And hedges his own way. But in this point
All his tricks founder, and he brings his physic
After his patient's death: the king already
Hath married the fair lady.

The king can now see how he deviously
follows his own path. But on this point
his tricks cannot work, and he brings his medicine
after the patient is dead: the King has already
married the fair lady.

SURREY
Would he had!

I wish he had!

SUFFOLK
May you be happy in your wish, my lord
For, I profess, you have it.

May your wish be granted, my lord,
I tell you it has been.

SURREY
Now, all my joy
Trace the conjunction!

May every happiness
bless the marriage!

SUFFOLK
My amen to't!

Amen to that!

NORFOLK
All men's!

So say all of us!

SUFFOLK
There's order given for her coronation:
Marry, this is yet but young, and may be left
To some ears unrecounted. But, my lords,
She is a gallant creature, and complete
In mind and feature: I persuade me, from her
Will fall some blessing to this land, which shall
In it be memorised.

An order has been passed for her coronation:
mind you, this has only just happened, so don't
spread it around. But, my lords,
she is a splendid creature, and perfect
in mind and body: I think that she
will bring some blessing for this country,
which will descend through the generations.

SURREY
But, will the king
Digest this letter of the cardinal's?
The Lord forbid!

But will the King
stomach the insult in this letter of the cardinal's?
Heaven forbid!

NORFOLK
Marry, amen!

Indeed, amen to that!

SUFFOLK
No, no;
There be moe wasps that buzz about his nose
Will make this sting the sooner. Cardinal Campeius
Is stol'n away to Rome; hath ta'en no leave;
Has left the cause o' the king unhandled; and
Is posted, as the agent of our cardinal,
To second all his plot. I do assure you
The king cried Ha! at this.

No, no;
there are other wasps buzzing around his nose
that will make him feel this sting earlier. Cardinal Campeius
has sneaked away to Rome; he said no goodbyes;
he has left the King's business undealt with; and
is seen as the agent of our cardinal,
who is his associate in this plot. I can assure you
the King was properly suspicious.

Chamberlain
Now, God incense him,
And let him cry Ha! louder!

Now, may God anger him,
and make him even more suspicious!

NORFOLK
But, my lord,
When returns Cranmer?

But, my lord,
when is Cranmer coming back?

SUFFOLK
He is return'd in his opinions; which
Have satisfied the king for his divorce,
Together with all famous colleges
Almost in Christendom: shortly, I believe,
His second marriage shall be publish'd, and
Her coronation. Katharine no more
Shall be call'd queen, but princess dowager
And widow to Prince Arthur.

He has sent back his advice; which
told the king his divorce was legitimate,
along with almost all the most famous
universities in Christendom: I believe that shortly
his second marriage shall be announced, and
her coronation. Katherine will no longer
be called Queen, but Princess Dowager
and widow of Prince Arthur.

NORFOLK
This same Cranmer's
A worthy fellow, and hath ta'en much pain
In the king's business.

This Cranmer
is a worthy fellow, and has taken much trouble
over the King's business.

SUFFOLK
He has; and we shall see him
For it an archbishop.

He has; and we shall see him
made an Archbishop for it.

NORFOLK
So I hear.

That's what I hear.

SUFFOLK
'Tis so.
The cardinal!

It's true.
Here's the cardinal!

Enter CARDINAL WOLSEY and CROMWELL

NORFOLK
Observe, observe, he's moody.

Look, look, he's moody.

CARDINAL WOLSEY
The packet, Cromwell.
Gave't you the king?

Did you give that packet
to the King, Cromwell?

CROMWELL
To his own hand, in's bedchamber.

Into his hands, in his bedroom.

CARDINAL WOLSEY
Look'd he o' the inside of the paper?

Did he look inside the letter?

CROMWELL
Presently
He did unseal them: and the first he view'd,
He did it with a serious mind; a heed
Was in his countenance. You he bade
Attend him here this morning.

He unsealed them
at once: and as soon as he read it
he became very serious; he looked
as though he thought deeply. He ordered
you to come to him here this morning.

CARDINAL WOLSEY
Is he ready
To come abroad?

Is he ready
to come out?

CROMWELL
I think, by this he is.

I think he is by this time.

CARDINAL WOLSEY
Leave me awhile.

Leave me for a while.

Exit CROMWELL

Aside

It shall be to the Duchess of Alencon,
The French king's sister: he shall marry her.
Anne Bullen! No; I'll no Anne Bullens for him:
There's more in't than fair visage. Bullen!
No, we'll no Bullens. Speedily I wish
To hear from Rome. The Marchioness of Pembroke!

It shall be to the Duchess of Alencon,
the sister of the French king: he shall marry her.
Anne Bullen! No; he shan't have Anne Bullen:

there are more important things than a pretty face. Bullen!
No, will have no more Bullens. I want to hear
from Rome soon. The Marchioness of Pembroke!

NORFOLK
He's discontented.

He's unhappy.

SUFFOLK
May be, he hears the king
Does whet his anger to him.

Maybe he's heard that the King
is getting angry with him.

SURREY
Sharp enough,
Lord, for thy justice!

May he be angry enough,
Lord, to carry out your justice!

CARDINAL WOLSEY
[Aside] The late queen's gentlewoman,
a knight's daughter,
To be her mistress' mistress! the queen's queen!
This candle burns not clear: 'tis I must snuff it;
Then out it goes. What though I know her virtuous
And well deserving? yet I know her for
A spleeny Lutheran; and not wholesome to
Our cause, that she should lie i' the bosom of
Our hard-ruled king. Again, there is sprung up
An heretic, an arch one, Cranmer; one
Hath crawl'd into the favour of the king,
And is his oracle.

The former queen's gentlewoman,
the daughter of a knight,
made the mistress of her mistress! The queen of a queen!
This is a dirty business and I'm the one who must
put a stop to it. So what if she is good
and well deserving? I still know she is
a devoted Lutheran; it would not be good
for our cause for her to have a place in the heart of
our hotheaded king. There's another one who's

sprung up, a heretic, a terrible one, Cranmer;
he has sneaked into the King's favour
and the King listens to his every word.

NORFOLK
He is vex'd at something.

He's upset about something.

SURREY
I would 'twere something that would fret the string,
The master-cord on's heart!

I hope it's something that will gnaw through
his heartstrings!

Enter KING HENRY VIII, reading of a schedule, and LOVELL

SUFFOLK
The king, the king!

The King, the King!

KING HENRY VIII
What piles of wealth hath he accumulated
To his own portion! and what expense by the hour
Seems to flow from him! How, i' the name of thrift,
Does he rake this together! Now, my lords,
Saw you the cardinal?

What enormous wealth he has gathered
for himself! How great his continual
expenditure seems to be! How, if he's thrifty,
has he managed to get such a pile! Now, my lords,
have you seen the cardinal?

Norfolk
My lord, we have
Stood here observing him: some strange commotion
Is in his brain: he bites his lip, and starts;
Stops on a sudden, looks upon the ground,
Then lays his finger on his temple, straight
Springs out into fast gait; then stops again,
Strikes his breast hard, and anon he casts
His eye against the moon: in most strange postures
We have seen him set himself.

My Lord, we have
been standing here watching him: there's some strange disturbance
in his brain: he bites his lip, and starts;
suddenly stops, looks at the ground,
then puts his finger on his forehead, immediately
starts walking quickly; then he stops again,
hits his chest hard, and then he looks
up at the moon: he has been putting himself
in the strangest positions.

King Henry VIII
It may well be,
There is a mutiny in's mind. This morning
Papers of state he sent me to peruse,
As I required: and wot you what I found
There,--on my conscience, put unwittingly?
Forsooth, an inventory, thus importing;
The several parcels of his plate, his treasure,
Rich stuffs, and ornaments of household; which
I find at such proud rate, that it out-speaks
Possession of a subject.

It might well be the case
that his mind is confused. This morning
he sent me state documents to read over,
as I had ordered: what do you think I found
there–I swear, put there accidentally?
I tell you, an inventory, showing this;
the amounts of his plate, his treasure,
his fine things and the furnishings of his household;
I find that he has so much, it's much more
than a subject ought to own.

NORFOLK
It's heaven's will:
Some spirit put this paper in the packet,
To bless your eye withal.

It's the will of heaven:
some spirit put the document in the packet,
to do you a favour.

KING HENRY VIII
If we did think
His contemplation were above the earth,

And fix'd on spiritual object, he should still
Dwell in his musings: but I am afraid
His thinkings are below the moon, not worth
His serious considering.

If I believed
his thoughts were above the Earth
and thinking of spiritual things, I wouldn't disturb
his meditation: but I'm afraid
he is thinking of worldly things, which
he shouldn't be wasting his time on.

King HENRY VIII takes his seat; whispers LOVELL, who goes to CARDINAL WOLSEY

CARDINAL WOLSEY
Heaven forgive me!
Ever God bless your highness!

Heaven forgive me!
May God always bless your Highness!

KING HENRY VIII
Good my lord,
You are full of heavenly stuff, and bear the inventory
Of your best graces in your mind; the which
You were now running o'er: you have scarce time
To steal from spiritual leisure a brief span
To keep your earthly audit: sure, in that
I deem you an ill husband, and am glad
To have you therein my companion.

My good lord,
you are full of the material of heaven, and have
a great store of the greatest virtues; that's what
you would have been thinking about: you hardly have time
to spare from your spiritual affairs
to keep inventory of things on earth: I must say that
makes you a bad manager, and makes me glad
to have you as my companion.

CARDINAL WOLSEY
Sir,
For holy offices I have a time; a time
To think upon the part of business which
I bear i' the state; and nature does require
Her times of preservation, which perforce

I, her frail son, amongst my brethren mortal,
Must give my tendence to.

Sir,
I have the time set aside for holy offices; a time
to think of the business which I undertake
for the state; and nature requires time
for rest, and as I am her frail son amongst
my mortal brothers I must obey her.

KING HENRY VIII
You have said well.

You have spoken well.

CARDINAL WOLSEY
And ever may your highness yoke together,
As I will lend you cause, my doing well
With my well saying!

And may your Highness always see,
as I give you reason to, that I back up
my good words with good deeds!

KING HENRY VIII
'Tis well said again;
And 'tis a kind of good deed to say well:
And yet words are no deeds. My father loved you:
He said he did; and with his deed did crown
His word upon you. Since I had my office,
I have kept you next my heart; have not alone
Employ'd you where high profits might come home,
But pared my present havings, to bestow
My bounties upon you.

You spoken well again;
and it's kind of a good deed to speak well:
but words are not deeds. My father loved you:
he said he did; and with his deeds he
confirmed his words. Since I have been king,
I have kept you close to my heart; I haven't only
used you in enterprises where there could be great profit
but reduced my own income in order to
be generous towards you.

CARDINAL WOLSEY

[Aside] What should this mean?

What does this mean?

SURREY
[Aside] The Lord increase this business!

May the Lord encourage this!

KING HENRY VIII
Have I not made you,
The prime man of the state? I pray you, tell me,
If what I now pronounce you have found true:
And, if you may confess it, say withal,
If you are bound to us or no. What say you?

Didn't I make you
the most important statesman in the country? Please, tell me,
if what I now tell you is true:
and, if you say it is, also say
if you are my servant or not. What do you say?

CARDINAL WOLSEY
My sovereign, I confess your royal graces,
Shower'd on me daily, have been more than could
My studied purposes requite; which went
Beyond all man's endeavours: my endeavours
Have ever come too short of my desires,
Yet filed with my abilities: mine own ends
Have been mine so that evermore they pointed
To the good of your most sacred person and
The profit of the state. For your great graces
Heap'd upon me, poor undeserver, I
Can nothing render but allegiant thanks,
My prayers to heaven for you, my loyalty,
Which ever has and ever shall be growing,
Till death, that winter, kill it.

My Lord, I confess that your royal favours,
showered upon me daily, have been more than
I could possibly repay; no man could
do enough to repay them: what I have done
has always been less than I wish to,
but the best I could do: all of my
endeavours have been geared towards
the best for your most sacred person and

the profit of the state. For the great favours
you have heaped on me, poor undeserving man, I
can only offer my loyal thanks,
my prayers to heaven for you, my loyalty,
which has always been and always will be growing
until the winter of death kills it.

KING HENRY VIII
Fairly answer'd;
A loyal and obedient subject is
Therein illustrated: the honour of it
Does pay the act of it; as, i' the contrary,
The foulness is the punishment. I presume
That, as my hand has open'd bounty to you,
My heart dropp'd love, my power rain'd honour, more
On you than any; so your hand and heart,
Your brain, and every function of your power,
Should, notwithstanding that your bond of duty,
As 'twere in love's particular, be more
To me, your friend, than any.

A good answer;
which shows you as
a loyal and obedient subject: the reward of loyalty
is the honour of being loyal; and, equally,
being disloyal is punishment in itself. I assume
that, as I have been generous with you
with goods, love, and honour, more to you
than any other, that your hand and heart,
your brain, and every part of your power
should, in spite of your duty to the Pope,
should, due to your intimate regard for me,
make me a greater friend   of you than any other.

CARDINAL WOLSEY
I do profess
That for your highness' good I ever labour'd
More than mine own; that am, have, and will be--
Though all the world should crack their duty to you,
And throw it from their soul; though perils did
Abound, as thick as thought could make 'em, and
Appear in forms more horrid,--yet my duty,
As doth a rock against the chiding flood,
Should the approach of this wild river break,
And stand unshaken yours.

I swear
that I have always worked more for the good
of your Highness than for me; that is and always shall be
(however much the rest of the world breaks its promises to you,
and rejects it from their soul; although danger could
surround me, as thick as thought could make it, and
in more horrible ways) my duty,
like a rock standing against the punishing flood,
if the wild river crashes against it,
I will remain steadfastly yours.

KING HENRY VIII
'Tis nobly spoken:
Take notice, lords, he has a loyal breast,
For you have seen him open't. Read o'er this;

Giving him papers

And after, this: and then to breakfast with
What appetite you have.

That's nobly spoken:
take note, Lords, that he has a loyal heart,
you have heard what he said. Read this;
[gives him papers]
and afterwards, this: and then go to breakfast with
whatever appetite you have.

Exit KING HENRY VIII, frowning upon CARDINAL WOLSEY: the Nobles throng after him,
smiling and whispering

CARDINAL WOLSEY
What should this mean?
What sudden anger's this? how have I reap'd it?
He parted frowning from me, as if ruin
Leap'd from his eyes: so looks the chafed lion
Upon the daring huntsman that has gall'd him;
Then makes him nothing. I must read this paper;
I fear, the story of his anger. 'Tis so;
This paper has undone me: 'tis the account
Of all that world of wealth I have drawn together
For mine own ends; indeed, to gain the popedom,
And fee my friends in Rome. O negligence!
Fit for a fool to fall by: what cross devil
Made me put this main secret in the packet

I sent the king? Is there no way to cure this?
No new device to beat this from his brains?
I know 'twill stir him strongly; yet I know
A way, if it take right, in spite of fortune
Will bring me off again. What's this? 'To the Pope!'
The letter, as I live, with all the business
I writ to's holiness. Nay then, farewell!
I have touch'd the highest point of all my greatness;
And, from that full meridian of my glory,
I haste now to my setting: I shall fall
Like a bright exhalation in the evening,
And no man see me more.

What does this mean?
What is this sudden anger? What have I done to deserve it?
He left me frowning, as if destruction
was leaping from his eyes: that's how the wounded lion
looks upon the daring huntsman who has injured him;
then destroys him. I must read this paper;
I'm afraid it will show why he is angry. I'm right,
this paper is my downfall: it's the account
of all the great wealth I have amassed
for my own purposes; in fact, to gain the title of Pope,
and to pay off my friends in Rome. What carelessness!
This is the way a fool would slip up: what angry devil
made me put this great secret in the packet
I sent to the King? Is there no way out of this?
No new trick to drive this out of his mind?
I know it will make him very angry; but I know
a way, if it works, that can get me back in his
good books despite this. What's this? 'To the Pope'?
By heaven, it's the letter with everything that I wrote
to his Holiness. No then, farewell:
I have reached the highest point of my greatness,
and from that great height of glory
I am now falling fast. I shall plummet
like a falling star in the evening,
and no one shall ever see me again.

Re-enter to CARDINAL WOLSEY, NORFOLK and SUFFOLK, SURREY, and the Chamberlain

NORFOLK
Hear the king's pleasure, cardinal: who commands you
To render up the great seal presently
Into our hands; and to confine yourself
To Asher House, my Lord of Winchester's,

Till you hear further from his highness.

Listen to the king's orders, cardinal: he orders you
to hand over the great seal at once
to me; and to remain at
Asher House, Lord Winchester's residence,
until you hear more from his Highness.

CARDINAL WOLSEY
Stay:
Where's your commission, lords? words cannot carry
Authority so weighty.

Wait:
where are your orders, lords? Words alone
cannot assume such authority.

SUFFOLK
Who dare cross 'em,
Bearing the king's will from his mouth expressly?

Who dares to disagree with them,
as they come directly from the King's mouth?

CARDINAL WOLSEY
Till I find more than will or words to do it,
I mean your malice, know, officious lords,
I dare and must deny it. Now I feel
Of what coarse metal ye are moulded, envy:
How eagerly ye follow my disgraces,
As if it fed ye! and how sleek and wanton
Ye appear in every thing may bring my ruin!
Follow your envious courses, men of malice;
You have Christian warrant for 'em, and, no doubt,
In time will find their fit rewards. That seal,
You ask with such a violence, the king,
Mine and your master, with his own hand gave me;
Bade me enjoy it, with the place and honours,
During my life; and, to confirm his goodness,
Tied it by letters-patents: now, who'll take it?

I will and I must deny it, until it is
backed up by more than strength or words,
for I know your malice towards me, officious lords.
Now I see that you are made of the base metal of malice:
how eagerly you pursue my disgrace,

as if it does you good! How quickly and energetically
you work for everything that can bring my ruin!
Follow your jealous paths, hateful men;
you have Christian excuses for them and, no doubt,
in time you will get your just reward. That seal,
which you demand with such violence, the King,
your master and mine, gave to me with his own hand;
he told me to enjoy it, with the position and honour which goes with it,
during my life; and, to confirm his goodness,
he gave me a contract for it. Now, who will take it?

SURREY
The king, that gave it.

The King who gave it.

CARDINAL WOLSEY
It must be himself, then.

He must do it himself, then.

SURREY
Thou art a proud traitor, priest.

You are an arrogant traitor, priest.

CARDINAL WOLSEY
Proud lord, thou liest:
Within these forty hours Surrey durst better
Have burnt that tongue than said so.

Arrogant lord, you are lying:
within the last forty hours you would have wished you had
burnt your tongue out rather than said that.

SURREY
Thy ambition,
Thou scarlet sin, robb'd this bewailing land
Of noble Buckingham, my father-in-law:
The heads of all thy brother cardinals,
With thee and all thy best parts bound together,
Weigh'd not a hair of his. Plague of your policy!
You sent me deputy for Ireland;
Far from his succor, from the king, from all
That might have mercy on the fault thou gavest him;
Whilst your great goodness, out of holy pity,

Absolved him with an axe.

Your ambition,
you scarlet sinner, robbed this unhappy land
of noble Buckingham, my father-in-law:
the heads of all your brother cardinals,
added together with you and all your best qualities
don't add up to a hair of his head. Damn your politics!
You sent me to be governor of Ireland,
where I couldn't help him, far from the King, from
anything that might have gained mercy for the sin you accused him of;
whilst in your great goodness, with your holy pity,
you forgave him with an axe.

CARDINAL WOLSEY
This, and all else
This talking lord can lay upon my credit,
I answer is most false. The duke by law
Found his deserts: how innocent I was
From any private malice in his end,
His noble jury and foul cause can witness.
If I loved many words, lord, I should tell you
You have as little honesty as honour,
That in the way of loyalty and truth
Toward the king, my ever royal master,
Dare mate a sounder man than Surrey can be,
And all that love his follies.

This, and anything else
this chattering lord blames on me,
I say is most false. The Duke got his
lawful punishment: his noble jury
and his foul behaviour are witness to
how innocent I was of any private malice.
If I loved talking, oh lord, I should tell you
that you are as dishonest as you are dishonourable,
and that in terms of loyalty and truth
towards the King, my always royal master,
I am a much better man than Surrey can be,
or any followers of his foolishness.

SURREY
By my soul,
Your long coat, priest, protects you; thou
shouldst feel
My sword i' the life-blood of thee else. My lords,

Can ye endure to hear this arrogance?
And from this fellow? if we live thus tamely,
To be thus jaded by a piece of scarlet,
Farewell nobility; let his grace go forward,
And dare us with his cap like larks.

Upon my soul,
your priestly robes protect you; otherwise you would feel
my sword inside you. My lords,
can you tolerate listening to this arrogance?
And from this fellow? If we live so meekly
that we can be cowed by a piece of scarlet cloth,
farewell to nobility; let his Grace carry on
and frighten us with his cap, like larks.

CARDINAL WOLSEY
All goodness
Is poison to thy stomach.

All goodness
is poisonous to you.

SURREY
Yes, that goodness
Of gleaning all the land's wealth into one,
Into your own hands, cardinal, by extortion;
The goodness of your intercepted packets
You writ to the pope against the king: your goodness,
Since you provoke me, shall be most notorious.
My Lord of Norfolk, as you are truly noble,
As you respect the common good, the state
Of our despised nobility, our issues,
Who, if he live, will scarce be gentlemen,
Produce the grand sum of his sins, the articles
Collected from his life. I'll startle you
Worse than the scaring bell, when the brown wench
Lay kissing in your arms, lord cardinal.

Yes, the goodness
of gathering the wealth of the whole land into one pile,
into your own hands, cardinal, through extortion;
the goodness of your intercepted letters
in which you wrote to the Pope against your king: your goodness,
since you have angered me, shall be notorious.
My Lord of Norfolk, as you are truly noble,
as you respect the common good, the state

of our despised nobility, our children,
who, if he lives, will hardly be even gentlemen,
take out the indictment, the charges
gathered from his life. I'll make you jump
more than the bell for morning service did, when you were lying
kissing a slut in your arms, lord cardinal.

CARDINAL WOLSEY
How much, methinks, I could despise this man,
But that I am bound in charity against it!

How much I could despise this man,
if I wasn't bound by charity not to!

NORFOLK
Those articles, my lord, are in the king's hand:
But, thus much, they are foul ones.

The charges, my lord, are held by the King:
but I can tell you this much, they are filthy ones.

CARDINAL WOLSEY
So much fairer
And spotless shall mine innocence arise,
When the king knows my truth.

So by contrast my innocence will appear
much fairer and more spotless
when the King knows the truth.

SURREY
This cannot save you:
I thank my memory, I yet remember
Some of these articles; and out they shall.
Now, if you can blush and cry 'guilty,' cardinal,
You'll show a little honesty.

This cannot save you:
thanks to my memory I can still remember
some of the charges; and they shall be revealed.
Now, cardinal, you could show a little honesty
by blushing and crying out 'I am guilty.'

CARDINAL WOLSEY
Speak on, sir;
I dare your worst objections: if I blush,

It is to see a nobleman want manners.

Go on, sir;
I can take your worst: if I blush,
it is because I can see a nobleman lacking in manners.

SURREY
I had rather want those than my head. Have at you!
First, that, without the king's assent or knowledge,
You wrought to be a legate; by which power
You maim'd the jurisdiction of all bishops.

I'd rather lack those than lack my head. Damn you!
Firstly you manoeuvred to become the Pope's representative
without the agreement or knowledge of the King;
and with that power you overthrew
the powers of all the bishops.

NORFOLK
Then, that in all you writ to Rome, or else
To foreign princes, 'Ego et Rex meus'
Was still inscribed; in which you brought the king
To be your servant.

Then, everything you wrote to Rome, or otherwise
to foreign princes, had 'my King and I'
still written on it; so you pretended
the King was your servant.

SUFFOLK
Then that, without the knowledge
Either of king or council, when you went
Ambassador to the emperor, you made bold
To carry into Flanders the great seal.

And also that without the knowledge
of the King or the council, when you went
as ambassador to the Emperor, you were so bold
as to take the great seal into Flanders.

SURREY
Item, you sent a large commission
To Gregory de Cassado, to conclude,
Without the king's will or the state's allowance,
A league between his highness and Ferrara.

As well, you sent a large commission
to Gregory de Cassado to arrange,
without permission from the King or the State,
an alliance between his Highness and Ferrara.

SUFFOLK
That, out of mere ambition, you have caused
Your holy hat to be stamp'd on the king's coin.

And, out of simple ambition, you issued coins
with your image in place of the King's.

SURREY
Then that you have sent innumerable substance--
By what means got, I leave to your own conscience--
To furnish Rome, and to prepare the ways
You have for dignities; to the mere undoing
Of all the kingdom. Many more there are;
Which, since they are of you, and odious,
I will not taint my mouth with.

And you have sent countless sums–
how you got them is a matter for your conscience–
to supply Rome and to help your plans
for advancement; causing the utter ruin
of the whole kingdom. There are many more charges;
which, since they involve you, and are hateful,
I will not sully my mouth with.

Chamberlain
O my lord,
Press not a falling man too far! 'tis virtue:
His faults lie open to the laws; let them,
Not you, correct him. My heart weeps to see him
So little of his great self.

O my Lord,
do not kick a man when he's down! It would be good:
his crimes shall be punished by the law; let the law,
* not you, do that. My heart weeps to see him*
in such reduced circumstances.

SURREY
I forgive him.

I forgive him.

SUFFOLK
Lord cardinal, the king's further pleasure is,
Because all those things you have done of late,
By your power legatine, within this kingdom,
Fall into the compass of a praemunire,
That therefore such a writ be sued against you;
To forfeit all your goods, lands, tenements,
Chattels, and whatsoever, and to be
Out of the king's protection. This is my charge.

Lord cardinal, the king further desires
that because all those things you have done recently
through your power from Rome, within this kingdom,
fall under the law against exercising Rome's power in England,
that a writ shall be issued against you,
to make you forfeit all your goods, lands, buildings,
movable property and anything else, and you shall
lose the protection of the King. These are my orders.

NORFOLK
And so we'll leave you to your meditations
How to live better. For your stubborn answer
About the giving back the great seal to us,
The king shall know it, and, no doubt, shall thank you.
So fare you well, my little good lord cardinal.

And now we'll leave you to think how you should
live a better life. The King shall be told
of your stubborn refusal to return the great seal to us,
and no doubt he will thank you for it.
So farewell, my good little lord cardinal.

Exeunt all but CARDINAL WOLSEY

CARDINAL WOLSEY
So farewell to the little good you bear me.
Farewell! a long farewell, to all my greatness!
This is the state of man: to-day he puts forth
The tender leaves of hopes; to-morrow blossoms,
And bears his blushing honours thick upon him;
The third day comes a frost, a killing frost,
And, when he thinks, good easy man, full surely
His greatness is a-ripening, nips his root,
And then he falls, as I do. I have ventured,

Like little wanton boys that swim on bladders,
This many summers in a sea of glory,
But far beyond my depth: my high-blown pride
At length broke under me and now has left me,
Weary and old with service, to the mercy
Of a rude stream, that must for ever hide me.
Vain pomp and glory of this world, I hate ye:
I feel my heart new open'd. O, how wretched
Is that poor man that hangs on princes' favours!
There is, betwixt that smile we would aspire to,
That sweet aspect of princes, and their ruin,
More pangs and fears than wars or women have:
And when he falls, he falls like Lucifer,
Never to hope again.

So farewell to the little good you wish me.
Farewell! A long farewell, to all my greatness!
This is the life of man: today he puts out
the tender leaves of his hopes; tomorrow he flowers,
and a multitude of honours decorate him;
on the third day there is a frost, a killing frost,
and just as he thinks, good gullible man, that his
greatness is surely ripening, it nips at his roots,
and then he falls, as I do. I have swum,
like the little careless boys who swim on bladders,
for many years in a sea of glory,
but far out of my depth: eventually my great pride
burst underneath me and has now left me,
tired and old with service, to the mercy
of a rough tide that will roll over me for ever.
Vain pomp and the glory of this world, I hate you:
I feel that my heart has been torn open. Oh, how wretched
the poor man who relies on the favours of Princes is!
Between the sweet smile of Princes which we hope for
and their anger lie more pain and anguish than
war or women can ever suffer:
and when a man falls, he falls like Lucifer,
and can never hope again.

Enter CROMWELL, and stands amazed

Why, how now, Cromwell!

Why, what is it, Cromwell!

CROMWELL

I have no power to speak, sir.

I've lost my power of speech, sir.

CARDINAL WOLSEY
What, amazed
At my misfortunes? can thy spirit wonder
A great man should decline? Nay, an you weep,
I am fall'n indeed.

What, astonished
by my misfortunes? Are you really amazed
that a great man can fall? No, if you weep,
I am truly fallen.

CROMWELL
How does your grace?

How is your Grace?

CARDINAL WOLSEY
Why, well;
Never so truly happy, my good Cromwell.
I know myself now; and I feel within me
A peace above all earthly dignities,
A still and quiet conscience. The king has cured me,
I humbly thank his grace; and from these shoulders,
These ruin'd pillars, out of pity, taken
A load would sink a navy, too much honour:
O, 'tis a burthen, Cromwell, 'tis a burthen
Too heavy for a man that hopes for heaven!

Why, I am well;
I have never been so truly happy, good Cromwell.
I know who I am now; and I feel inside me
a peace greater than all earthly honours,
an easy and quiet conscience. The King has cured me,
I humbly thank his grace; out of pity he has taken
away from these shoulders, these ruined pillars,
a weight that could sink a Navy, too much honour:
oh, it's a burden, Cromwell, it's a burden
too heavy for a man who hopes to go to heaven!

CROMWELL
I am glad your grace has made that right use of it.

I'm glad to see your Grace looking at it that way.

CARDINAL WOLSEY
I hope I have: I am able now, methinks,
Out of a fortitude of soul I feel,
To endure more miseries and greater far
Than my weak-hearted enemies dare offer.
What news abroad?

I hope I am: I think that I am now able
through the strength of soul that I feel
to endure far greater misery, and more of it,
and my weak hearted enemies can offer me.
What news is going round?

CROMWELL
The heaviest and the worst
Is your displeasure with the king.

The worst and most serious
is your trouble with the king.

CARDINAL WOLSEY
God bless him!

God bless him!

CROMWELL
The next is, that Sir Thomas More is chosen
Lord chancellor in your place.

The next is, that Sir Thomas More has been chosen
as Lord Chancellor in your place.

CARDINAL WOLSEY
That's somewhat sudden:
But he's a learned man. May he continue
Long in his highness' favour, and do justice
For truth's sake and his conscience; that his bones,
When he has run his course and sleeps in blessings,
May have a tomb of orphans' tears wept on em! What more?

That's rather sodden:
but he's an educated man. May he remain
in his Highness' favour for a long time, and do the right thing
for the sake of truth and his conscience; so that his bones,

when his life has run out and he gains blessed sleep,
may be covered with the tears of orphans! What else?

CROMWELL
That Cranmer is return'd with welcome,
Install'd lord archbishop of Canterbury.

Cranmer has been welcomed back,
and made Lord Archbishop of Canterbury.

CARDINAL WOLSEY
That's news indeed.

That's certainly news.

CROMWELL
Last, that the Lady Anne,
Whom the king hath in secrecy long married,
This day was view'd in open as his queen,
Going to chapel; and the voice is now
Only about her coronation.

Lastly that the Lady Anne,
who has been secretly married to the King for a long time,
was today seen out in the open as his Queen,
going to chapel; and all the gossip is now
about her coronation.

CARDINAL WOLSEY
There was the weight that pull'd me down. O Cromwell,
The king has gone beyond me: all my glories
In that one woman I have lost for ever:
No sun shall ever usher forth mine honours,
Or gild again the noble troops that waited
Upon my smiles. Go, get thee from me, Cromwell;
I am a poor fall'n man, unworthy now
To be thy lord and master: seek the king;
That sun, I pray, may never set! I have told him
What and how true thou art: he will advance thee;
Some little memory of me will stir him--
I know his noble nature--not to let
Thy hopeful service perish too: good Cromwell,
Neglect him not; make use now, and provide
For thine own future safety.

That was the weight that pulled me down. Oh Cromwell,

the King is lost to me; through that one woman
I have lost all my glory forever:
no sun shall ever shine again on my honours,
or on the crowds of followers who waited
for my approval. Go away from me, Cromwell;
I am a fallen man, unworthy now
of being your lord and master: find the king;
I pray that that sun may never set! I have told him
who you are and how loyal you are: he will promote you;
some small memory of me will motivate him—
I know his noble nature—to allow your
good services to be rewarded: good Cromwell,
do not ignore him; use him now, and solidify
your position for the future.

CROMWELL
O my lord,
Must I, then, leave you? must I needs forego
So good, so noble and so true a master?
Bear witness, all that have not hearts of iron,
With what a sorrow Cromwell leaves his lord.
The king shall have my service: but my prayers
For ever and for ever shall be yours.

O my Lord,
then must I leave you? Do I need to abandon
such a good, noble and true master?
All who do not have hearts of iron please witness
how sadly Cromwell leaves his Lord.
I shall serve the King: but my prayers
will be yours for ever.

CARDINAL WOLSEY
Cromwell, I did not think to shed a tear
In all my miseries; but thou hast forced me,
Out of thy honest truth, to play the woman.
Let's dry our eyes: and thus far hear me, Cromwell;
And, when I am forgotten, as I shall be,
And sleep in dull cold marble, where no mention
Of me more must be heard of, say, I taught thee,
Say, Wolsey, that once trod the ways of glory,
And sounded all the depths and shoals of honour,
Found thee a way, out of his wreck, to rise in;
A sure and safe one, though thy master miss'd it.
Mark but my fall, and that that ruin'd me.
Cromwell, I charge thee, fling away ambition:

By that sin fell the angels; how can man, then,
The image of his Maker, hope to win by it?
Love thyself last: cherish those hearts that hate thee;
Corruption wins not more than honesty.
Still in thy right hand carry gentle peace,
To silence envious tongues. Be just, and fear not:
Let all the ends thou aim'st at be thy country's,
Thy God's, and truth's; then if thou fall'st,
O Cromwell,
Thou fall'st a blessed martyr! Serve the king;
And,--prithee, lead me in:
There take an inventory of all I have,
To the last penny; 'tis the king's: my robe,
And my integrity to heaven, is all
I dare now call mine own. O Cromwell, Cromwell!
Had I but served my God with half the zeal
I served my king, he would not in mine age
Have left me naked to mine enemies.

Cromwell, I did not think I would cry
in all my misery; but you have made me,
through your honest truth, act like a woman.
Let's dry our eyes; and at least listen to this,
and when I am forgotten, as I will be,
and sleeping in my tomb, when I shall
never be mentioned again, say I taught you;
say Wolsey, who once trod the paths of glory,
and sailed across all the oceans of honour,
found a way when he was shipwrecked for you to rise,
a sure and safe way, although your master missed it.
Just take note of my fall, and what ruined me:
Cromwell, I order you, throw away ambition,
the sin that made the Angels fall; so how can man,
the image of his maker, hope to profit by it?
Love yourself last of all, love those who hate you;
honesty does better than corruption.
Always carry gentle peace with you
to silence jealous tongues. Be just, and don't be afraid;
let everything you do be for the good of the country,
God and truth: and if you fall, O Cromwell,
you will fall as a blessed martyr.
Serve the King: and please take me in:
take an inventory of all my possessions,
to the last penny, it belongs to the king. My robe,
and my loyalty to heaven, is all
I can now call my own. Oh, Cromwell, Cromwell.

If I had served my God with half the enthusiasm
with which I served my king, he would not have left me
naked to my enemies in my old age.

CROMWELL
Good sir, have patience.

Good sir, have patience.

CARDINAL WOLSEY
So I have. Farewell
The hopes of court! my hopes in heaven do dwell.

I have. Farewell
to the ambitions of court! My hope lives in heaven.

Exeunt

Act IV

SCENE I. A street in Westminster.

Enter two Gentlemen, meeting one another

First Gentleman
You're well met once again.

Good to see you again.

Second Gentleman
So are you.

The same to you.

First Gentleman
You come to take your stand here, and behold
The Lady Anne pass from her coronation?

Have you come to stand here and watch
Lady Anne on her way from her coronation?

Second Gentleman
'Tis all my business. At our last encounter,
The Duke of Buckingham came from his trial.

That's what I'm here for. Last time we met,
the Duke of Buckingham was coming from his trial.

First Gentleman
'Tis very true: but that time offer'd sorrow;
This, general joy.

That's very true, but that was a sorrowful time;
this is a time of general happiness.

Second Gentleman
'Tis well: the citizens,
I am sure, have shown at full their royal minds--
As, let 'em have their rights, they are ever forward--
In celebration of this day with shows,
Pageants and sights of honour.

It's good: the citizens
have certainly shown their fondness for royalty—
as, to give them their due, they always do—
by celebrating this day with shows,
pageants and great displays.

First Gentleman
Never greater,
Nor, I'll assure you, better taken, sir.

There never have been greater,
nor, I can assure you, more welcome, sir.

Second Gentleman
May I be bold to ask at what that contains,
That paper in your hand?

Might I be so bold as to enquire what
that paper in your hand says?

First Gentleman
Yes; 'tis the list
Of those that claim their offices this day
By custom of the coronation.
The Duke of Suffolk is the first, and claims
To be high-steward; next, the Duke of Norfolk,
He to be earl marshal: you may read the rest.

Yes, it is the list
of those who claim their titles today
as is customary at the coronation.
The Duke of Suffolk is the first, he claims
the right of being high Steward; next comes the Duke of Norfolk,
he shall be Earl Marshall: you may read the rest.

Second Gentleman
I thank you, sir: had I not known those customs,
I should have been beholding to your paper.
But, I beseech you, what's become of Katharine,
The princess dowager? how goes her business?

Thank you, Sir: if I didn't know these customs,
your paper would have been very useful.
But, I must ask you, what happened to Katherine,
the Princess Dowager? How goes it with her?

First Gentleman
That I can tell you too. The Archbishop
Of Canterbury, accompanied with other
Learned and reverend fathers of his order,
Held a late court at Dunstable, six miles off
From Ampthill where the princess lay; to which
She was often cited by them, but appear'd not:
And, to be short, for not appearance and
The king's late scruple, by the main assent
Of all these learned men she was divorced,
And the late marriage made of none effect
Since which she was removed to Kimbolton,
Where she remains now sick.

I can tell you that too. The Archbishop
of Canterbury, accompanied by other
learned and reverend fathers of his order,
recently held a court at Dunstable, six miles away
from Ampthill where the Princess was staying;
they often summoned her, but she did not come:
and, to cut a long story short, because she didn't appear
and because of the King's recent doubts, she was
divorced by a unanimous vote of all these learned men,
and her previous marriage was declared invalid.
Since then she has gone to Kimbolton,
where she is now lying ill.

Second Gentleman
Alas, good lady!

Alas, good lady!

Trumpets

The trumpets sound: stand close, the queen is coming.

The trumpets are sounding: stand close to me, the Queen is coming.

Hautboys

THE ORDER OF THE CORONATION

1. A lively flourish of Trumpets.
2. Then, two Judges.
3. Lord Chancellor, with the purse and mace
before him.

4. Choristers, singing.

Music

5. Mayor of London, bearing the mace. Then
Garter, in his coat of arms, and on his
head a gilt copper crown.
6. Marquess Dorset, bearing a sceptre of gold,
on his head a demi-coronal of gold. With
him, SURREY, bearing the rod of silver with
the dove, crowned with an earl's coronet.
Collars of SS.
7. SUFFOLK, in his robe of estate, his coronet
on his head, bearing a long white wand, as
high-steward. With him, NORFOLK, with the
rod of marshalship, a coronet on his head.
Collars of SS.
8. A canopy borne by four of the Cinque-ports;
under it, QUEEN ANNE in her robe; in her hair
richly adorned with pearl, crowned. On each
side her, the Bishops of London and
Winchester.
9. The old Duchess of Norfolk, in a coronal of
gold, wrought with flowers, bearing QUEEN
ANNE's train.
10. Certain Ladies or Countesses, with plain
circlets of gold without flowers.

They pass over the stage in order and state

Second Gentleman
A royal train, believe me. These I know:
Who's that that bears the sceptre?

*A royal procession, I'll swear. I know these people,
who is that who's carrying the sceptre?*

First Gentleman
Marquess Dorset:
And that the Earl of Surrey, with the rod.

*The Marquess Dorset:
and that's the Earl of Surrey, carrying the rod.*

Second Gentleman
A bold brave gentleman. That should be

150

The Duke of Suffolk?

A bold brave gentleman. Is that
the Duke of Suffolk?

First Gentleman
'Tis the same: high-steward.

That's him: high Steward.

Second Gentleman
And that my Lord of Norfolk?

And that's my Lord of Norfolk?

First Gentleman
Yes;

Yes.

Second Gentleman
Heaven bless thee!

Looking on QUEEN ANNE

Thou hast the sweetest face I ever look'd on.
Sir, as I have a soul, she is an angel;
Our king has all the Indies in his arms,
And more and richer, when he strains that lady:
I cannot blame his conscience.

Heaven bless you!
You have the sweetest face I ever saw.
Sir, upon my soul, she is an angel;
our King possesses something more valuable
than the whole of the Indies when he embraces that lady:
I can't blame him for wanting her.

First Gentleman
They that bear
The cloth of honour over her, are four barons
Of the Cinque-ports.

Those who carry
the canopy over her are four Barons
of the Cinque ports.

Second Gentleman
Those men are happy; and so are all are near her.
I take it, she that carries up the train
Is that old noble lady, Duchess of Norfolk.

Those men are lucky; and so all who are near her.
I take it that the one who is carrying the train
is that old noble lady, Duchess of Norfolk.

First Gentleman
It is; and all the rest are countesses.

It is; and all the rest are Countesses.

Second Gentleman
Their coronets say so. These are stars indeed;
And sometimes falling ones.

I can see by their coronets. These are certainly stars;
and sometimes they fall.

First Gentleman
No more of that.

That's enough of that.

Exit procession, and then a great flourish of trumpets

Enter a third Gentleman

First Gentleman
God save you, sir! where have you been broiling?

God save you, sir! Where have you been sweating?

Third Gentleman
Among the crowd i' the Abbey; where a finger
Could not be wedged in more: I am stifled
With the mere rankness of their joy.

Amongst the crowd in the Abbey; you couldn't have got
another finger in there: I am choked
with the stench of their joy.

Second Gentleman

You saw
The ceremony?

You saw
the ceremony?

Third Gentleman
That I did.

I certainly did.

First Gentleman
How was it?

How was it?

Third Gentleman
Well worth the seeing.

Well worth seeing.

Second Gentleman
Good sir, speak it to us.

Good sir, describe it to us.

Third Gentleman
As well as I am able. The rich stream
Of lords and ladies, having brought the queen
To a prepared place in the choir, fell off
A distance from her; while her grace sat down
To rest awhile, some half an hour or so,
In a rich chair of state, opposing freely
The beauty of her person to the people.
Believe me, sir, she is the goodliest woman
That ever lay by man: which when the people
Had the full view of, such a noise arose
As the shrouds make at sea in a stiff tempest,
As loud, and to as many tunes: hats, cloaks--
Doublets, I think,--flew up; and had their faces
Been loose, this day they had been lost. Such joy
I never saw before. Great-bellied women,
That had not half a week to go, like rams
In the old time of war, would shake the press,
And make 'em reel before 'em. No man living
Could say 'This is my wife' there; all were woven

So strangely in one piece.

As well as I can. The rich stream
of lords and ladies, having brought the Queen
to a prepared place in the choir, retreated
some distance from her; then her Grace sat down
to rest for a while, some half an hour or so,
on a rich throne, exposing her beauty
freely to the people.
Believe me sir, she is the most beautiful woman
as ever slept with a man: and when the people
had a full view of her, such a noise rose up
that was like the sails of a ship in a stiff wind,
just as loud, with as many different noises. Hats, cloaks
shirts too, I think, flew up, and if their faces could have come off
they would have lost them today. I never saw
such joy before. Great round bellied women,
with just half a week to go before giving birth, smashed
into the crowd like battering rams in old battles,
and made the everyone fall before them. No man alive
could have identified his wife in there, everyone was
entwined as if they were a single organism.

Second Gentleman
But, what follow'd?

But what happened after that?

Third Gentleman
At length her grace rose, and with modest paces
Came to the altar; where she kneel'd, and saint-like
Cast her fair eyes to heaven and pray'd devoutly.
Then rose again and bow'd her to the people:
When by the Archbishop of Canterbury
She had all the royal makings of a queen;
As holy oil, Edward Confessor's crown,
The rod, and bird of peace, and all such emblems
Laid nobly on her: which perform'd, the choir,
With all the choicest music of the kingdom,
Together sung 'Te Deum.' So she parted,
And with the same full state paced back again
To York-place, where the feast is held.

Eventually her grace arose, and with modest steps
came to the altar; she knelt there, and like a saint
turned her fair face up to heaven and prayed devoutly.

Then she got up again and bowed to her people:
then the Archbishop Canterbury
gave her all the royal trappings of a Queen,
such as holy oil, the Crown of Edward the Confessor,
the rod, bird of peace, and all the other symbols
which sat nobly on her: and the choir performed
all the best music of the kingdom,
then sang the Te Deum together. So she left,
and in the same majestic trappings walked back again
to York Place, where the feast is being held.

First Gentleman
Sir,
You must no more call it York-place, that's past;
For, since the cardinal fell, that title's lost:
'Tis now the king's, and call'd Whitehall.

Sir,
you mustn't call it York Place any more, that's gone;
for, since the downfall of the cardinal, that title's lost:
it now belongs to the King, and it's called Whitehall.

Third Gentleman
I know it;
But 'tis so lately alter'd, that the old name
Is fresh about me.

I know that;
but it's been so recently changed that the old name
still lingers in my memory.

Second Gentleman
What two reverend bishops
Were those that went on each side of the queen?

Who were those two reverend bishops
on each side of the Queen?

Third Gentleman
Stokesly and Gardiner; the one of Winchester,
Newly preferr'd from the king's secretary,
The other, London.

Stokesley and Gardiner; one Bishop of Winchester,
recently promoted from being the King's secretary,
the other is Bishop of London.

Second Gentleman
He of Winchester
Is held no great good lover of the archbishop's,
The virtuous Cranmer.

The Bishop of Winchester
is said to be no great friend of the Archbishop,
the virtuous Cranmer.

Third Gentleman
All the land knows that:
However, yet there is no great breach; when it comes,
Cranmer will find a friend will not shrink from him.

The whole country knows that:
however, they have not yet had any great argument; when it comes,
Cranmer will find a friend who will stand by him.

Second Gentleman
Who may that be, I pray you?

Who would that be, may I ask?

Third Gentleman
Thomas Cromwell;
A man in much esteem with the king, and truly
A worthy friend. The king has made him master
O' the jewel house,
And one, already, of the privy council.

Thomas Cromwell;
a man very much in the King's favour, and truly
a worthy friend. The King has made him master
of the Crown Jewels,
and already a member of the privy Council.

Second Gentleman
He will deserve more.

He'll get more than this.

Third Gentleman
Yes, without all doubt.
Come, gentlemen, ye shall go my way, which
Is to the court, and there ye shall be my guests:

Something I can command. As I walk thither,
I'll tell ye more.

Yes, doubtless.
Come, gentlemen, you shall come with me as
I go to the court, and you shall be my guests there:
I have the right to ask that. As we walk there
I'll tell you more.

Both
You may command us, sir.

We are both at your command, sir.

Exeunt

SCENE II. Kimbolton.

Enter KATHARINE, Dowager, sick; led between GRIFFITH, her gentleman usher, and PATIENCE, her woman

GRIFFITH
How does your grace?

How is your grace?

KATHARINE
O Griffith, sick to death!
My legs, like loaden branches, bow to the earth,
Willing to leave their burthen. Reach a chair:
So; now, methinks, I feel a little ease.
Didst thou not tell me, Griffith, as thou led'st me,
That the great child of honour, Cardinal Wolsey, was dead?

O Griffin, I am sick to death!
My legs, like heavily laden branches, bow down to the earth,
wanting to shed their load. Pull up a chair:
there; now, I think, I feel a little better.
Didn't you tell me, Griffith, as you led me,
that the great honourable Cardinal Wolsey was dead?

GRIFFITH
Yes, madam; but I think your grace,
Out of the pain you suffer'd, gave no ear to't.

Yes, madam; but I thought your grace
had not heard me due to the pain you were suffering.

KATHARINE
Prithee, good Griffith, tell me how he died:
If well, he stepp'd before me, happily
For my example.

Please, good Griffith, tell me how he died:
if he died well, he did better than me, perhaps
I could use him for an example.

GRIFFITH

Well, the voice goes, madam:
For after the stout Earl Northumberland
Arrested him at York, and brought him forward,
As a man sorely tainted, to his answer,
He fell sick suddenly, and grew so ill
He could not sit his mule.

Well, the rumour goes, madam,
that after the good Royal Northumberland
arrested him at York, and brought him down
for his trial as a badly suspected man
he suddenly fell sick, and became so ill
he could not sit on his mule.

KATHARINE
Alas, poor man!

Alas, poor man!

GRIFFITH
At last, with easy roads, he came to Leicester,
Lodged in the abbey; where the reverend abbot,
With all his covent, honourably received him;
To whom he gave these words, 'O, father abbot,
An old man, broken with the storms of state,
Is come to lay his weary bones among ye;
Give him a little earth for charity!'
So went to bed; where eagerly his sickness
Pursued him still: and, three nights after this,
About the hour of eight, which he himself
Foretold should be his last, full of repentance,
Continual meditations, tears, and sorrows,
He gave his honours to the world again,
His blessed part to heaven, and slept in peace.

At last, in small stages, he came to Leicester,
where he stayed in the Abbey; the reverend abbot,
with all his convent, received him honourably;
and he spoke these words to him, 'Oh, father abbot,
an old man, broken by the storms of politics,
has come to lay down his weary bones amongst you;
be so kind as to give him a little place to be buried.'
So he went to bed; and his illness became
worse: and, three nights later,
about eight o'clock, the time which he himself
had predicted would see his end, full of repentance,

religious thoughts, tears and sorrows,
he gave his honours back to the world,
his soul to heaven, and slept in peace.

KATHARINE
So may he rest; his faults lie gently on him!
Yet thus far, Griffith, give me leave to speak him,
And yet with charity. He was a man
Of an unbounded stomach, ever ranking
Himself with princes; one that, by suggestion,
Tied all the kingdom: simony was fair-play;
His own opinion was his law: i' the presence
He would say untruths; and be ever double
Both in his words and meaning: he was never,
But where he meant to ruin, pitiful:
His promises were, as he then was, mighty;
But his performance, as he is now, nothing:
Of his own body he was ill, and gave
The clergy in example.

And may he rest in peace; may his faults not punish him too much!
But let me say this about him, Griffith,
speaking kindly. He was a man
of unparalleled greed, who thought he was
as high as a prince; someone who through underhand methods
enslaved the whole kingdom: corruption was acceptable to him;
his own opinion was law: he would lie
in the presence of the King; and everything he said
had a double meaning: he never showed pity
except where he intended destruction:
his promises, like him, were mighty,
but as he is now they came to nothing:
he was physically depraved and set
a bad example for the clergy.

GRIFFITH
Noble madam,
Men's evil manners live in brass; their virtues
We write in water. May it please your highness
To hear me speak his good now?

Noble madam,
the evil manners of men are engraved on brass,
their goodness is written on water. Would your Highness allow
me to speak well of him now?

KATHARINE
Yes, good Griffith;
I were malicious else.

Yes, good Griffith;
otherwise I would be unkind.

GRIFFITH
This cardinal,
Though from an humble stock, undoubtedly
Was fashion'd to much honour from his cradle.
He was a scholar, and a ripe and good one;
Exceeding wise, fair-spoken, and persuading:
Lofty and sour to them that loved him not;
But to those men that sought him sweet as summer.
And though he were unsatisfied in getting,
Which was a sin, yet in bestowing, madam,
He was most princely: ever witness for him
Those twins Of learning that he raised in you,
Ipswich and Oxford! one of which fell with him,
Unwilling to outlive the good that did it;
The other, though unfinish'd, yet so famous,
So excellent in art, and still so rising,
That Christendom shall ever speak his virtue.
His overthrow heap'd happiness upon him;
For then, and not till then, he felt himself,
And found the blessedness of being little:
And, to add greater honours to his age
Than man could give him, he died fearing God.

This cardinal,
though from humble stock, was undoubtedly
marked out for honour. From birth
he was a scholar, and a very good one,
exceedingly wise, well spoken and persuasive:
he was haughty and sour to those who did not love him,
but to those men who wanted to be friends, he was sweet as summer.
And although he was certainly greedy
–which was a sin–but he was also princely in his
generosity: that will always be witnessed
by those two colleges he established,
at Ipswich and Oxford; one of them fell with him,
unwilling to outlive the goodness that built it,
the other, though unfinished, is already so famous,
so excellent in learning and still growing reputation,
that Christendom will forever speak of his goodness.

His downfall was a source of great happiness to him,
for then he realised who he was, as he never had before,
and found how blessed it is to be of no importance;
and to give him greater honour in his old age
than any man could give him, he died fearing God.

KATHARINE
After my death I wish no other herald,
No other speaker of my living actions,
To keep mine honour from corruption,
But such an honest chronicler as Griffith.
Whom I most hated living, thou hast made me,
With thy religious truth and modesty,
Now in his ashes honour: peace be with him!
Patience, be near me still; and set me lower:
I have not long to trouble thee. Good Griffith,
Cause the musicians play me that sad note
I named my knell, whilst I sit meditating
On that celestial harmony I go to.

After my death I do not wish any other Herald,
nobody to speak about what I did in my life,
to keep my honour from corruption,
I just want an honest chronicler like Griffith.
You have made me, with your religious truth
and modesty, honour the ashes of the one whom I
most hated when he was alive: may he rest in peace!
Be patient, stay with me; let me lie down more:
I won't bother you for long. Good Griffith,
ask the musicians to play that sad tune
which I chose as my death knell, whilst I
contemplate the heavenly music I'll be hearing soon.

Sad and solemn music

GRIFFITH
She is asleep: good wench, let's sit down quiet,
For fear we wake her: softly, gentle Patience.

She is asleep: good lady, let's sit down quietly
and make sure we don't wake her: quietly, gentle Patience.

The vision. Enter, solemnly tripping one after another, six personages, clad in white robes, wearing on their heads garlands of bays, and golden vizards on their faces; branches of bays or palm in their hands. They first congee unto her, then dance; and, at certain changes, the first two hold a spare garland over her head; at which the other four make reverent curtsies; then the two that held the garland deliver the same to the other next two, who observe the same order in their changes, and holding the garland over her head: which done, they deliver the same garland to the last two, who likewise observe the same order: at which, as it were by inspiration, she makes in her sleep signs of rejoicing, and holdeth up her hands to heaven: and so in their dancing vanish, carrying the garland with them. The music continues

KATHARINE
Spirits of peace, where are ye? are ye all gone,
And leave me here in wretchedness behind ye?

Spirits of peace, where have you gone? Have you all gone,
and left me here in wretchedness behind you?

GRIFFITH
Madam, we are here.

Madam, we are here.

KATHARINE
It is not you I call for:
Saw ye none enter since I slept?

It's not you I'm calling for:
didn't you see anyone come in since I went to sleep?

GRIFFITH
None, madam.

Nobody, madam.

KATHARINE
No? Saw you not, even now, a blessed troop
Invite me to a banquet; whose bright faces
Cast thousand beams upon me, like the sun?
They promised me eternal happiness;
And brought me garlands, Griffith, which I feel
I am not worthy yet to wear: I shall, assuredly.

No? Didn't you see, just now, a blessed band
invite me to a banquet; their bright faces
shining a thousand beams on me, like the sun?
They promised me eternal happiness;

and they brought me garlands, Griffith, which I feel
I am not yet worthy to wear: I certainly shall in future.

GRIFFITH
I am most joyful, madam, such good dreams
Possess your fancy.

It makes me very happy, madam,
that you are having such sweet dreams.

KATHARINE
Bid the music leave,
They are harsh and heavy to me.

Tell the musicians to stop,
it sounds harsh and heavy to me now.

Music ceases

PATIENCE
Do you note
How much her grace is alter'd on the sudden?
How long her face is drawn? how pale she looks,
And of an earthy cold? Mark her eyes!

Do you see
how much her grace has changed all of a sudden?
How drawn her face has become? How pale she looks,
and as cold as earth? Look in her eyes!

GRIFFITH
She is going, wench: pray, pray.

She is going, girl: pray, pray.

PATIENCE
Heaven comfort her!

May Heaven comfort her!

Enter a Messenger

Messenger
An't like your grace,--

If it pleases your Grace–

KATHARINE
You are a saucy fellow:
Deserve we no more reverence?

You are cheeky fellow:
don't I deserve more respect?

GRIFFITH
You are to blame,
Knowing she will not lose her wonted greatness,
To use so rude behavior; go to, kneel.

You should not be so rude
as to treat her any way differently to when she was Queen;
get down on your knees.

Messenger
I humbly do entreat your highness' pardon;
My haste made me unmannerly. There is staying
A gentleman, sent from the king, to see you.

I humbly beg your Highness' pardon;
my haste made me ill mannered. A gentleman
from the King is waiting to see you.

KATHARINE
Admit him entrance, Griffith: but this fellow
Let me ne'er see again.

Exeunt GRIFFITH and Messenger
Re-enter GRIFFITH, with CAPUCIUS
If my sight fail not,
You should be lord ambassador from the emperor,
My royal nephew, and your name Capucius.

Let him in, Griffith: but I never want to
see this fellow again.

If my eyes do not deceive me,
you are the lord ambassador from the Emperor,
my royal nephew, and your name is Capucius.

CAPUCIUS
Madam, the same; your servant.

Madam, I am him; at your service.

KATHARINE
O, my lord,
The times and titles now are alter'd strangely
With me since first you knew me. But, I pray you,
What is your pleasure with me?

Oh, my lord,
the times and titles have now been strangely altered
for me since you first knew me. But, please,
what do you want with me?

CAPUCIUS
Noble lady,
First mine own service to your grace; the next,
The king's request that I would visit you;
Who grieves much for your weakness, and by me
Sends you his princely commendations,
And heartily entreats you take good comfort.

Noble lady,
firstly I want to offer my services to your grace;
also the King requested that I visit you;
he is very sorry for your illness, and through me
sends you his princely greetings,
and heartily begs you to be of good cheer.

KATHARINE
O my good lord, that comfort comes too late;
'Tis like a pardon after execution:
That gentle physic, given in time, had cured me;
But now I am past all comforts here, but prayers.
How does his highness?

Oh my good lord, his comfort comes too late;
it's like a pardon after an execution:
that sweet medicine, given in time, would have cured me;
but now I am past all comfort apart from prayers.
How is his Highness?

CAPUCIUS
Madam, in good health.

Madam, he is in good health.

KATHARINE
So may he ever do! and ever flourish,
When I shal l dwell with worms, and my poor name
Banish'd the kingdom! Patience, is that letter,
I caused you write, yet sent away?

I hope he always will be! May he always prosper,
when I am living with the worms, and my poor name
has been banned from the kingdom! Patience, is that letter,
which I told you to write, sent yet?

PATIENCE
No, madam.

No, madam.

Giving it to KATHARINE

KATHARINE
Sir, I most humbly pray you to deliver
This to my lord the king.

Sir, I most humbly request that you deliver
this to my lord the king.

CAPUCIUS
Most willing, madam.

Certainly, madam.

KATHARINE
In which I have commended to his goodness
The model of our chaste loves, his young daughter;
The dews of heaven fall thick in blessings on her!
Beseeching him to give her virtuous breeding--
She is young, and of a noble modest nature,
I hope she will deserve well,--and a little
To love her for her mother's sake, that loved him,
Heaven knows how dearly. My next poor petition
Is, that his noble grace would have some pity
Upon my wretched women, that so long
Have follow'd both my fortunes faithfully:
Of which there is not one, I dare avow,
And now I should not lie, but will deserve
For virtue and true beauty of the soul,
For honesty and decent carriage,

A right good husband, let him be a noble
And, sure, those men are happy that shall have 'em.
The last is, for my men; they are the poorest,
But poverty could never draw 'em from me;
That they may have their wages duly paid 'em,
And something over to remember me by:
If heaven had pleased to have given me longer life
And able means, we had not parted thus.
These are the whole contents: and, good my lord,
By that you love the dearest in this world,
As you wish Christian peace to souls departed,
Stand these poor people's friend, and urge the king
To do me this last right.

In it I have asked him to kindly take care of
the image of our perfect love, his young daughter–
May Heaven pour down blessings upon her–
asking him to give her a good upbringing
–she is young and of a noble modest nature,
I hope she turns out well–and to love her
a little for her mother's sake, who loved him,
God knows how much. My next poor request
is that his noble grace should have some pity
on my wretched women, who have for so long
stayed with me whatever happened to me,
and I swear that there isn't one
(and I would not lie now) who does not deserve,
due to the goodness and beauty of their souls,
their honesty and decent behaviour,
a proper good husband (let him be a nobleman)
and it's certain that they will make those who have them happy.
The last request is for my men, they are very poor
(but they would never leave me due to poverty)
and I would like their wages properly paid to them,
with something over to remember me by.
If heaven had chosen to give me a longer life
and sufficient means, we would not part like this.
That's all I have to say, and my good lord,
by all that you love most in the world,
as you wish dead souls to find Christian peace,
be a friend to these poor people, and urge the King
to do this last thing for me.

CAPUCIUS
By heaven, I will,
Or let me lose the fashion of a man.

By heaven, I will,
or let me lose the title of man.

KATHARINE
I thank you, honest lord. Remember me
In all humility unto his highness:
Say his long trouble now is passing
Out of this world; tell him, in death I bless'd him,
For so I will. Mine eyes grow dim. Farewell,
My lord. Griffith, farewell. Nay, Patience,
You must not leave me yet: I must to bed;
Call in more women. When I am dead, good wench,
Let me be used with honour: strew me over
With maiden flowers, that all the world may know
I was a chaste wife to my grave: embalm me,
Then lay me forth: although unqueen'd, yet like
A queen, and daughter to a king, inter me.
I can no more.

I thank you, good lord. Give his Highness
my most humble respects:
so the one who caused him such trouble is now
leaving this world; tell him that I blessed him as I died,
for I shall do so. My eyes are growing dim. Farewell,
my lord. Griffith, farewell. No, Patience,
you must not leave me yet: I must go to bed;
call more women in. When I'm dead, good girl,
treat me with respect: cover me over
with maidenly flowers, so that all the world will know
that I was a pure wife to my grave: embalm me,
then lay me out for burial: although my title has been taken away,
Bury me like a queen, and the daughter of the King.
I can say no more.

Exeunt, leading KATHARINE

Act V

SCENE I. London. A gallery in the palace.

Enter GARDINER, Bishop of Winchester, a Page with a torch before him, met by LOVELL

GARDINER
It's one o'clock, boy, is't not?

It's one o'clock, boy, isn't it?

Boy
It hath struck.

It has struck.

GARDINER
These should be hours for necessities,
Not for delights; times to repair our nature
With comforting repose, and not for us
To waste these times. Good hour of night, Sir Thomas!
Whither so late?

These hours should be spent on essentials,
not on pleasure; it's time to restore our nature
with sweet sleep, not to waste
these hours. Good evening, Sir Thomas!
Where are you going so late?

LOVELL
Came you from the king, my lord?

Did you come from the King, my lord?

GARDINER
I did, Sir Thomas: and left him at primero
With the Duke of Suffolk.

I did, Sir Thomas: I left him playing primero
with the Duke of Suffolk.

LOVELL
I must to him too,
Before he go to bed. I'll take my leave.

I must go to him too,
before he goes to bed. I shall leave you.

GARDINER
Not yet, Sir Thomas Lovell. What's the matter?
It seems you are in haste: an if there be
No great offence belongs to't, give your friend
Some touch of your late business: affairs, that walk,
As they say spirits do, at midnight, have
In them a wilder nature than the business
That seeks dispatch by day.

Not yet, Sir Thomas Lovell. What's the matter?
It seems you are in a hurry: and if it won't
cause any offence, tell your friend
what you're up to: business that's conducted
at midnight, like the business of ghosts,
is wilder than the business
that is done in the day.

LOVELL
My lord, I love you;
And durst commend a secret to your ear
Much weightier than this work. The queen's in labour,
They say, in great extremity; and fear'd
She'll with the labour end.

My lord, I love you;
and I would trust you with a secret
much greater than this one. The Queen is in labour,
they say she is in great difficulty and it's feared
that she will die in childbirth.

GARDINER
The fruit she goes with
I pray for heartily, that it may find
Good time, and live: but for the stock, Sir Thomas,
I wish it grubb'd up now.

I pray heartily for
the fruit she will bear, and hope it will
survive: but for the tree, Sir Thomas,
I would like it to be grubbed up now.

LOVELL

Methinks I could
Cry the amen; and yet my conscience says
She's a good creature, and, sweet lady, does
Deserve our better wishes.

I think I could
say amen to that; but my conscience says
she's a good creature, and, sweet lady,
deserves good wishes from us.

GARDINER
But, sir, sir,
Hear me, Sir Thomas: you're a gentleman
Of mine own way; I know you wise, religious;
And, let me tell you, it will ne'er be well,
'Twill not, Sir Thomas Lovell, take't of me,
Till Cranmer, Cromwell, her two hands, and she,
Sleep in their graves.

But, sir, sir,
listen to me, Sir Thomas: you're a gentleman
after my own heart; I know you to be wise and religious;
and, let me tell you, nothing will ever come to any good,
it will not, Sir Thomas Lovell, believe you me,
until Cranmer and Cromwell, her two hands, and her,
sleep in their graves.

LOVELL
Now, sir, you speak of two
The most remark'd i' the kingdom. As for Cromwell,
Beside that of the jewel house, is made master
O' the rolls, and the king's secretary; further, sir,
Stands in the gap and trade of moe preferments,
With which the time will load him. The archbishop
Is the king's hand and tongue; and who dare speak
One syllable against him?

Now, sir, you're talking about two
of the most notable men in the kingdom. As for Cromwell,
as well as being master of the jewel house he has been made master
of the rolls, and the King's secretary; and, Sir,
he stands in a position to receive more promotions
which he will gain in time. The Archbishop
is the king's right-hand man and mouthpiece; who dares to say
one word against him?

GARDINER
Yes, yes, Sir Thomas,
There are that dare; and I myself have ventured
To speak my mind of him: and indeed this day,
Sir, I may tell it you, I think I have
Incensed the lords o' the council, that he is,
For so I know he is, they know he is,
A most arch heretic, a pestilence
That does infect the land: with which they moved
Have broken with the king; who hath so far
Given ear to our complaint, of his great grace
And princely care foreseeing those fell mischiefs
Our reasons laid before him, hath commanded
To-morrow morning to the council-board
He be convented. He's a rank weed, Sir Thomas,
And we must root him out. From your affairs
I hinder you too long: good night, Sir Thomas.

Yes, yes, Sir Thomas,
there are those who dare; and I myself have risked
speaking my mind about him: and indeed today,
Sir, I can tell you, I think I have
convinced the lords of the Council that he is,
as I know he is, and they know he is,
a terrible heretic, a disease
who infects the country: they have shared
their anger with the King; he has listened
to our complaint to the extent that, with his great grace
and princely care observing the evil mischief
which we told him was coming, has ordered
the board of the council to meet tomorrow morning
to summon him. He's a dirty weed, Sir Thomas,
and we must root out. I'm keeping you too long
from your business: good night, Sir Thomas.

LOVELL
Many good nights, my lord: I rest your servant.

Many good nights, my lord: I remain your servant.

Exeunt GARDINER and Page

Enter KING HENRY VIII and SUFFOLK

KING HENRY VIII
Charles, I will play no more tonight;

My mind's not on't; you are too hard for me.

Charles, I won't play any more tonight;
my mind is not on it; you are too much for me to handle.

SUFFOLK
Sir, I did never win of you before.

Sir, I never won from you before.

KING HENRY VIII
But little, Charles;
Nor shall not, when my fancy's on my play.
Now, Lovell, from the queen what is the news?

It was only a little, Charles;
and you shan't again, when my mind is on the game.
Now, Lovell, what news from the queen?

LOVELL
I could not personally deliver to her
What you commanded me, but by her woman
I sent your message; who return'd her thanks
In the great'st humbleness, and desired your highness
Most heartily to pray for her.

I couldn't personally give her
the message you ordered me to take, but
one of her women passed it along; she returned
her most humble thanks, and asked your Highness
to pray for her most heartily.

KING HENRY VIII
What say'st thou, ha?
To pray for her? what, is she crying out?

What are you saying, hey?
To pray for her? What, is she screaming?

LOVELL
So said her woman; and that her sufferance made
Almost each pang a death.

That's what her woman said; and the pain made
every contraction like death.

KING HENRY VIII
Alas, good lady!

Alas, good lady!

SUFFOLK
God safely quit her of her burthen, and
With gentle travail, to the gladding of
Your highness with an heir!

May God take her burden from her safely
and gently, to please your
Highness with an heir!

KING HENRY VIII
'Tis midnight, Charles;
Prithee, to bed; and in thy prayers remember
The estate of my poor queen. Leave me alone;
For I must think of that which company
Would not be friendly to.

It's midnight, Charles;
please, go to bed; and remember the condition
of my poor Queen in your prayers. Leave me alone;
for I must think of things which
are not suitable for company.

SUFFOLK
I wish your highness
A quiet night; and my good mistress will
Remember in my prayers.

I wish your highness
a restful night; and I shall remember my
good mistress in my prayers.

KING HENRY VIII
Charles, good night.

Charles, good night.

Exit SUFFOLK

Enter DENNY

Well, sir, what follows?

Well, Sir, what's going on?

DENNY
Sir, I have brought my lord the archbishop,
As you commanded me.

So, I have brought my lord the Archbishop,
as you ordered me.

KING HENRY VIII
Ha! Canterbury?

Ha! Canterbury?

DENNY
Ay, my good lord.

Yes, my good lord.

KING HENRY VIII
'Tis true: where is he, Denny?

That's good: where is he, Denny?

DENNY
He attends your highness' pleasure.

He is awaiting your Highness' pleasure.

Exit DENNY

LOVELL
[Aside] This is about that which the bishop spake:
I am happily come hither.

This concerns the matter which the bishop spoke of:
it's lucky I'm here.

Re-enter DENNY, with CRANMER

KING HENRY VIII
Avoid the gallery.

LOVELL seems to stay

Ha! I have said. Be gone. What?

Leave the gallery.

Ha! I've told you. Go. What?

Exeunt LOVELL and DENNY

CRANMER
[Aside]
I am fearful: wherefore frowns he thus?
'Tis his aspect of terror. All's not well.

I'm afraid: why is he frowning like that?
That's his terrifying expression. Something is wrong.

KING HENRY VIII
How now, my lord! you desire to know
Wherefore I sent for you.

Hello there, my lord! You want to know
why I sent for you.

CRANMER
[Kneeling] It is my duty
To attend your highness' pleasure.

It is my duty
to come when your Highness calls.

KING HENRY VIII
Pray you, arise,
My good and gracious Lord of Canterbury.
Come, you and I must walk a turn together;
I have news to tell you: come, come, give me your hand.
Ah, my good lord, I grieve at what I speak,
And am right sorry to repeat what follows
I have, and most unwillingly, of late
Heard many grievous, I do say, my lord,
Grievous complaints of you; which, being consider'd,
Have moved us and our council, that you shall
This morning come before us; where, I know,
You cannot with such freedom purge yourself,
But that, till further trial in those charges
Which will require your answer, you must take
Your patience to you, and be well contented

To make your house our Tower: you a brother of us,
It fits we thus proceed, or else no witness
Would come against you.

Please, get up,
my good and gracious Lord of Canterbury.
Come, you and I must walk a little together;
I have news to tell you: come, give me your hand.
Ah, my good lord, I am sorry to have to say this,
truly sorry to have to repeat that I have
recently, most unwillingly, heard many grievous
complaints against you; having looked at them
I and my council have decided that you shall
appear before us in the morning; I know that
you will not be able to completely clear yourself there,
but you will have to be patient until you can face
further trials on those charges which will demand
your answer, and you will have to be satisfied
with being confined to your house: this is
the appropriate way to proceed, as you are so close to me,
otherwise no witnesses would ever come forward.

CRANMER
[Kneeling]
I humbly thank your highness;
And am right glad to catch this good occasion
Most throughly to be winnow'd, where my chaff
And corn shall fly asunder: for, I know,
There's none stands under more calumnious tongues
Than I myself, poor man.

I humbly thank your Highness;
and I'm very glad to have this chance
to be thoroughly tested, and for all
the wheat to be separated from the chaff: for, I know,
there is nobody who is so unjustly gossiped about
as myself, poor man.

KING HENRY VIII
Stand up, good Canterbury:
Thy truth and thy integrity is rooted
In us, thy friend: give me thy hand, stand up:
Prithee, let's walk. Now, by my holidame.
What manner of man are you? My lord, I look'd
You would have given me your petition, that
I should have ta'en some pains to bring together

Yourself and your accusers; and to have heard you,
Without indurance, further.

Stand up, good Canterbury:
your truth and your integrity are not
doubted by me, your friend: give me your hand, stand up:
please, let's walk. Now, by our Lady,
what sort of man are you? My lord, I thought
you would have begged me to
arrange a meeting between yourself
and your accusers; and to have done this
without any further imprisonment.

CRANMER
Most dread liege,
The good I stand on is my truth and honesty:
If they shall fail, I, with mine enemies,
Will triumph o'er my person; which I weigh not,
Being of those virtues vacant. I fear nothing
What can be said against me.

My feared Lord,
I rely on my truth and honesty:
if they fail I will join with my enemies
in my downfall; I don't care about that,
if I don't have those virtues. I'm afraid of nothing
that can be said against me.

KING HENRY VIII
Know you not
How your state stands i' the world, with the whole world?
Your enemies are many, and not small; their practises
Must bear the same proportion; and not ever
The justice and the truth o' the question carries
The due o' the verdict with it: at what ease
Might corrupt minds procure knaves as corrupt
To swear against you? such things have been done.
You are potently opposed; and with a malice
Of as great size. Ween you of better luck,
I mean, in perjured witness, than your master,
Whose minister you are, whiles here he lived
Upon this naughty earth? Go to, go to;
You take a precipice for no leap of danger,
And woo your own destruction.

Do you not know

what your position is in the world, with the whole world?
Your enemies are numerous, and not lowborn; their plots
must be of a proportionate size; the justice
and truth of a case does not always match up with
the verdict; how easily might
corrupt minds hire scoundrels just as corrupt
to give evidence against you? These things have been done before.
You have powerful enemies; and their malice
matches their size. I hope you have better luck
in this matter of perjured witnesses than your master,
whose minister you are, when he lived here
on this wicked Earth. Come on, man;
you are walking along the edge of the precipice for no reason,
risking your own destruction.

CRANMER
God and your majesty
Protect mine innocence, or I fall into
The trap is laid for me!

May God and your Majesty
protect my innocence, or I shall fall into
the trap that has been set for me!

KING HENRY VIII
Be of good cheer;
They shall no more prevail than we give way to.
Keep comfort to you; and this morning see
You do appear before them: if they shall chance,
In charging you with matters, to commit you,
The best persuasions to the contrary
Fail not to use, and with what vehemency
The occasion shall instruct you: if entreaties
Will render you no remedy, this ring
Deliver them, and your appeal to us
There make before them. Look, the good man weeps!
He's honest, on mine honour. God's blest mother!
I swear he is true--hearted; and a soul
None better in my kingdom. Get you gone,
And do as I have bid you.

Exit CRANMER

He has strangled
His language in his tears.

Don't worry;
they shall have no more success than I allow.
Be comforted; and in the morning make sure
that you appear before them: if they happen
when putting charges against you to commit you to the Tower,
do not fail to use all the best arguments against it you have,
with whatever passion seems appropriate at the time:
if your pleading is unsuccessful, show them
this ring, and tell them you appealed to me.
Look, the good man is weeping:
I swear that he's honest. By the Blessed mother of God,
I swear he is true hearted, and that there isn't
a better soul in my kingdom. Off you go,
and do as I have told you.
He can't speak for tears.

Enter Old Lady, LOVELL following

Gentleman
[Within] Come back: what mean you?

Come back: what are you up to?

Old Lady
I'll not come back; the tidings that I bring
Will make my boldness manners. Now, good angels
Fly o'er thy royal head, and shade thy person
Under their blessed wings!

I shan't come back; the news that I bring
gives me licence to be bold. Now, may good angels
fly over your royal head, and shade your person
under their blessed wings!

KING HENRY VIII
Now, by thy looks
I guess thy message. Is the queen deliver'd?
Say, ay; and of a boy.

Now, I can guess your message
from your looks. Has the Queen given birth?
Say yes, and say it is a boy.

Old Lady
Ay, ay, my liege;
And of a lovely boy: the God of heaven

Both now and ever bless her! 'tis a girl,
Promises boys hereafter. Sir, your queen
Desires your visitation, and to be
Acquainted with this stranger 'tis as like you
As cherry is to cherry.

Yes, yes, my lord;
and a lovely boy: the God of heaven
bless her now and always! It's a girl,
which promises boys afterwards. Sir, your Queen
wants to see you, and to
introduce you to this stranger who is as like you
as one cherry to another.

KING HENRY VIII
Lovell!

Lovell!

LOVELL
Sir?

Sir?

KING HENRY VIII
Give her an hundred marks. I'll to the queen.

Give her a hundred marks. I'll go to the Queen.

Exit

Old Lady
An hundred marks! By this light, I'll ha' more.
An ordinary groom is for such payment.
I will have more, or scold it out of him.
Said I for this, the girl was like to him?
I will have more, or else unsay't; and now,
While it is hot, I'll put it to the issue.

A hundred marks! I swear I shall have more.
An ordinary groom would be paid this much.
I will have more, or I shall nag it out of him.
Is it for this that I said the girl was like him?
I'll have more, or I'll take it back; and now,
I'll strike while the iron is hot.

Exeunt

SCENE II. Before the council-chamber. Pursuivants, Pages, & c. attending.

Enter CRANMER

CRANMER
I hope I am not too late; and yet the gentleman,
That was sent to me from the council, pray'd me
To make great haste. All fast? what means this? Ho!
Who waits there? Sure, you know me?

I hope I'm not too late; and yet the gentleman,
who was sent to me from the council, begged me
to hurry. All locked up? What does this mean? Hello!
Who's there? Surely, you know me?

Enter Keeper
Keeper
Yes, my lord;
But yet I cannot help you.

Yes, my lord;
but still I can't help you.

CRANMER
Why?

Why not?

Enter DOCTOR BUTTS

Keeper
Your grace must wait till you be call'd for.

Your Grace must wait until you're called for.

CRANMER
So.

Very well.

DOCTOR BUTTS

[Aside] This is a piece of malice. I am glad
I came this way so happily: the king
Shall understand it presently.

*This is done maliciously. I am glad
I had the luck to come this way: the King
shall learn about this at once.*

Exit

CRANMER
[Aside] 'Tis Butts,
The king's physician: as he pass'd along,
How earnestly he cast his eyes upon me!
Pray heaven, he sound not my disgrace! For certain,
This is of purpose laid by some that hate me--
God turn their hearts! I never sought their malice--
To quench mine honour: they would shame to make me
Wait else at door, a fellow-counsellor,
'Mong boys, grooms, and lackeys. But their pleasures
Must be fulfill'd, and I attend with patience.

*It's Butts,
the King's doctor: as he passed by,
what a strange look he gave me!
Please heaven, let him not see my disgrace! It's certain
that this has been done deliberately by people who hate me–
I wish they'd change their feelings, I never did them any harm–
to damage my honour: otherwise they'd be ashamed to make me
wait at the door, a fellow councillor,
amongst the boys, grooms and lackeys. But they must
get what they want, and I shall wait patiently.*

Enter the KING HENRY VIII and DOCTOR BUTTS at a window above

DOCTOR BUTTS
I'll show your grace the strangest sight--

I'll show you will grace the strangest sight–

KING HENRY VIII
What's that, Butts?

What's that, Butts?

DOCTOR BUTTS

I think your highness saw this many a day.

That I think your Highness has seen a long time.

KING HENRY VIII
Body o' me, where is it?

By my body, where is it?

DOCTOR BUTTS
There, my lord:
The high promotion of his grace of Canterbury;
Who holds his state at door, 'mongst pursuivants,
Pages, and footboys.

There, my lord:
your great Archbishop of Canterbury;
holding his position at the door, amongst heralds,
pages and footmen.

KING HENRY VIII
Ha! 'tis he, indeed:
Is this the honour they do one another?
'Tis well there's one above 'em yet. I had thought
They had parted so much honesty among 'em
At least, good manners, as not thus to suffer
A man of his place, and so near our favour,
To dance attendance on their lordships' pleasures,
And at the door too, like a post with packets.
By holy Mary, Butts, there's knavery:
Let 'em alone, and draw the curtain close:
We shall hear more anon.

Ha! It certainly is him:
is this the way they are each other?
It's a good job there is still someone higher than them. I thought
they at least had enough honesty amongst them,
or good manners, not to force
a man of his position, so liked by me,
to hang around waiting for their Lordships' permission,
and at the door too, like a postman with letters.
By holy Mary, Butts, that's skullduggery:
leave them to it, and close the curtains tight:
we'll hear more about this soon.

Exeunt

SCENE III. The Council-Chamber.

Enter Chancellor; places himself at the upper end of the table on the left hand; a seat being left void above him, as for CRANMER's seat. SUFFOLK, NORFOLK, SURREY, Chamberlain, GARDINER, seat themselves in order on each side. CROMWELL at lower end, as secretary. Keeper at the door

Chancellor
Speak to the business, master-secretary:
Why are we met in council?

Speak to the purpose, Master Secretary:
why have we met in Council?

CROMWELL
Please your honours,
The chief cause concerns his grace of Canterbury.

If it please your Honours,
the main reason is to do with his grace of Canterbury.

GARDINER
Has he had knowledge of it?

Has he been informed about it?

CROMWELL
Yes.

Yes.

NORFOLK
Who waits there?

Who's that waiting there?

Keeper
Without, my noble lords?

Outside, my noble Lords?

GARDINER

Yes.

Yes.

Keeper
My lord archbishop;
And has done half an hour, to know your pleasures.

My Lord Archbishop;
he has been waiting half an hour, to know what you want.

Chancellor
Let him come in.

Let him come in.

Keeper
Your grace may enter now.

Your Grace may enter now.

CRANMER enters and approaches the council-table

Chancellor
My good lord archbishop, I'm very sorry
To sit here at this present, and behold
That chair stand empty: but we all are men,
In our own natures frail, and capable
Of our flesh; few are angels: out of which frailty
And want of wisdom, you, that best should teach us,
Have misdemean'd yourself, and not a little,
Toward the king first, then his laws, in filling
The whole realm, by your teaching and your chaplains,
For so we are inform'd, with new opinions,
Divers and dangerous; which are heresies,
And, not reform'd, may prove pernicious.

My good Lord Archbishop, I'm very sorry
to have to sit here now, and see
your chair standing empty: but we are all men,
our nature is weak, and can often be ruled
by the flesh; few of us are angels: and because of this weakness
and lack of wisdom, you, who should set an example,
have behaved badly, and not in a small way,
firstly towards the King, and then to his laws, by filling
the whole country, through your teaching and your chaplains,

so we are told, with new opinions,
perverse and dangerous; they are heresies,
and, if they are not withdrawn, they may prove very damaging.

GARDINER
Which reformation must be sudden too,
My noble lords; for those that tame wild horses
Pace 'em not in their hands to make 'em gentle,
But stop their mouths with stubborn bits, and spur 'em,
Till they obey the manage. If we suffer,
Out of our easiness and childish pity
To one man's honour, this contagious sickness,
Farewell all physic: and what follows then?
Commotions, uproars, with a general taint
Of the whole state: as, of late days, our neighbours,
The upper Germany, can dearly witness,
Yet freshly pitied in our memories.

And they must be withdrawn at once too,
my noble lords; people who tame wild horses
don't exercise them gently with their hands,
but block up their mouths with hard bits, and dig in the spurs,
until they do as they're told. If we allow,
by being easy-going and having a childish regard
for one man's honour, this infectious sickness to spread,
then any cure will be useless: and what will happen then?
Riots, uproar, and general corruption
throughout the country: as, recently, our neighbours
in upper Germany have found to their cost,
we still remember and pity them.

CRANMER
My good lords, hitherto, in all the progress
Both of my life and office, I have labour'd,
And with no little study, that my teaching
And the strong course of my authority
Might go one way, and safely; and the end
Was ever, to do well: nor is there living,
I speak it with a single heart, my lords,
A man that more detests, more stirs against,
Both in his private conscience and his place,
Defacers of a public peace, than I do.
Pray heaven, the king may never find a heart
With less allegiance in it! Men that make
Envy and crooked malice nourishment
Dare bite the best. I do beseech your lordships,

That, in this case of justice, my accusers,
Be what they will, may stand forth face to face,
And freely urge against me.

My good lords, thus far, in everything I've done
in my life and my post, I have endeavoured,
with no little effort, for my teaching
and the strong use of my power
to both be consistent, and good; my aim
was always to do good: and there is no man living,
I can say wholeheartedly, my lords,
no one who hates more, or works harder to stop,
both in private life and as a public figure,
disturbers of the public peace, than me.
I pray to God that the King will always have
such faithful hearts around him! Men who derive
nourishment from envy and crooked malice
are the first to criticise it. I beg your Lordships,
as this is a judicial case, that my accusers,
whoever they are, come out and face me,
and speak their accusations against me openly.

SUFFOLK
Nay, my lord,
That cannot be: you are a counsellor,
And, by that virtue, no man dare accuse you.

No, my lord,
that can't happen: you are a counsellor,
and, because of that, no man dares to accuse you.

GARDINER
My lord, because we have business of more moment,
We will be short with you. 'Tis his highness' pleasure,
And our consent, for better trial of you,
From hence you be committed to the Tower;
Where, being but a private man again,
You shall know many dare accuse you boldly,
More than, I fear, you are provided for.

My Lord, because we have more important business,
we will be brief with you. His Highness wishes,
and we agree to it, that in order for you to be better tried
you should be taken from here and imprisoned in the Tower;
where, becoming only a private citizen again,
you will know how many make accusations against you,

more than you're expecting, I'm afraid.

CRANMER
Ah, my good Lord of Winchester, I thank you;
You are always my good friend; if your will pass,
I shall both find your lordship judge and juror,
You are so merciful: I see your end;
'Tis my undoing: love and meekness, lord,
Become a churchman better than ambition:
Win straying souls with modesty again,
Cast none away. That I shall clear myself,
Lay all the weight ye can upon my patience,
I make as little doubt, as you do conscience
In doing daily wrongs. I could say more,
But reverence to your calling makes me modest.

Ah, my good lord Winchester, thank you;
you are always a good friend to me; if you get what you want,
I shall find your lordship both judge and jury,
you are so merciful: I see your plan:
you want my downfall: love and meekness, Lord,
are more suitable to a clergyman than ambition:
win back souls who stray from the path by modesty,
do not reject any. I am certain that I shall exonerate
myself, however much you test me, I have as little doubt
as you have conscience in the daily wrongs you do.
I could say more, but respect for your position
curbs my tongue.

GARDINER
My lord, my lord, you are a sectary,
That's the plain truth: your painted gloss discovers,
To men that understand you, words and weakness.

My Lord, my lord, you are a follower of a sect,
that's the simple truth: this outward display shows,
to men who understand you, just empty words and weakness.

CROMWELL
My Lord of Winchester, you are a little,
By your good favour, too sharp; men so noble,
However faulty, yet should find respect
For what they have been: 'tis a cruelty
To load a falling man.

My Lord Winchester, you are a little,

if you'll excuse me saying so, too sharp; such noble men,
whatever their faults, should still be given respect
for what they once were: it's cruel
to kick a man when he's down.

GARDINER
Good master secretary,
I cry your honour mercy; you may, worst
Of all this table, say so.

Good Master Secretary,
I beg your honour to excuse me; you have
the least right of everyone at this table to say that.

CROMWELL
Why, my lord?

Why, my lord?

GARDINER
Do not I know you for a favourer
Of this new sect? ye are not sound.

Don't I know that you follow
this new sect? You are not trustworthy.

CROMWELL
Not sound?

Not trustworthy?

GARDINER
Not sound, I say.

Not trustworthy, I say.

CROMWELL
Would you were half so honest!
Men's prayers then would seek you, not their fears.

I wish you were half as honest as me!
Then men would pray to you, not fear you.

GARDINER
I shall remember this bold language.

I shall remember this intemperate language.

CROMWELL
Do.
Remember your bold life too.

Do.
Remember your intemperate life too.

Chancellor
This is too much;
Forbear, for shame, my lords.

That's enough;
stop this, for shame, my lords.

GARDINER
I have done.

I'm finished.

CROMWELL
And I.

So am I.

Chancellor
Then thus for you, my lord: it stands agreed,
I take it, by all voices, that forthwith
You be convey'd to the Tower a prisoner;
There to remain till the king's further pleasure
Be known unto us: are you all agreed, lords?

So we must deal with you, my lord: it's agreed,
I take it, unanimously, that now you should be
taken to the Tower as a prisoner;
to remain there until the King's further orders
are given to us: are you all agreed, Lords?

All
We are.

We are.

CRANMER
Is there no other way of mercy,

But I must needs to the Tower, my lords?

Is there nothing else you can do
apart from send me to the Tower, my lords?

GARDINER
What other
Would you expect? you are strangely troublesome.
Let some o' the guard be ready there.

What else
do you expect? You're being extremely annoying.
Bring some of the guards in there.

Enter Guard

CRANMER
For me?
Must I go like a traitor thither?

For me?
Must I go there like a traitor?

GARDINER
Receive him,
And see him safe i' the Tower.

Take him,
and put him safely in the Tower.

CRANMER
Stay, good my lords,
I have a little yet to say. Look there, my lords;
By virtue of that ring, I take my cause
Out of the gripes of cruel men, and give it
To a most noble judge, the king my master.

Wait, my good lords,
I still have a little I want to say. Look at this, my lords;
through the power of this ring, I take my case
out of the grip of cruel men, and place it
before a most noble judge, my master the king.

Chamberlain
This is the king's ring.

This is the king's ring.

SURREY
'Tis no counterfeit.

It's not a fake.

SUFFOLK
'Tis the right ring, by heaven: I told ye all,
When ye first put this dangerous stone a-rolling,
'Twould fall upon ourselves.

I swear, it's the true ring: I told you all,
when you first started this dangerous stone rolling,
that it would fall on us.

NORFOLK
Do you think, my lords,
The king will suffer but the little finger
Of this man to be vex'd?

Do you think, my lords,
that the King will allow just one little finger
of this man to be harmed?

Chancellor
'Tis now too certain:
How much more is his life in value with him?
Would I were fairly out on't!

That's now obvious:
so how much more valuable will his life be to him?
I wish I was out of this business!

CROMWELL
My mind gave me,
In seeking tales and informations
Against this man, whose honesty the devil
And his disciples only envy at,
Ye blew the fire that burns ye: now have at ye!

I had my suspicions,
that in looking for gossip and information
against this man, whose honesty makes
the devil and his disciples envious,
that you were stoking the fire that would burn you: now you're for it!

Enter KING, frowning on them; takes his seat

GARDINER
Dread sovereign, how much are we bound to heaven
In daily thanks, that gave us such a prince;
Not only good and wise, but most religious:
One that, in all obedience, makes the church
The chief aim of his honour; and, to strengthen
That holy duty, out of dear respect,
His royal self in judgment comes to hear
The cause betwixt her and this great offender.

Mighty King, we give heaven thanks
every day for giving us such a prince;
not only good and wise, but also most religious:
one who, with all obedience, makes the church
the central pillar of his honour; and, to enhance
that holy duty, out of sweet respect,
he has come himself to judge the case
between the church and this great offender.

KING HENRY VIII
You were ever good at sudden commendations,
Bishop of Winchester. But know, I come not
To hear such flattery now, and in my presence;
They are too thin and bare to hide offences.
To me you cannot reach, you play the spaniel,
And think with wagging of your tongue to win me;
But, whatsoe'er thou takest me for, I'm sure
Thou hast a cruel nature and a bloody.

You were always good at off-the-cuff compliments,
Bishop of Winchester. But you should know, I have not come
here to hear such flattery to my face;
it's too threadbare to hide your offences.
You act towards me like a spaniel, to me who is so much higher than you,
and think that you can win me over with your words;
but, whoever you think I am, I'm certain
that your nature is cruel and bloody.

To CRANMER

Good man, sit down. Now let me see the proudest
He, that dares most, but wag his finger at thee:
By all that's holy, he had better starve

Than but once think this place becomes thee not.

Good man, sit down. Now let me see the most arrogant man,
the most daring, just point his finger at you:
by all that is holy, he would be better off starving
than to even think you don't deserve your place here.

SURREY
May it please your grace,--

If your Grace pleases–

KING HENRY VIII
No, sir, it does not please me.
I had thought I had had men of some understanding
And wisdom of my council; but I find none.
Was it discretion, lords, to let this man,
This good man,--few of you deserve that title,--
This honest man, wait like a lousy footboy
At chamber--door? and one as great as you are?
Why, what a shame was this! Did my commission
Bid ye so far forget yourselves? I gave ye
Power as he was a counsellor to try him,
Not as a groom: there's some of ye, I see,
More out of malice than integrity,
Would try him to the utmost, had ye mean;
Which ye shall never have while I live.

No, sir, I am not pleased.
I thought I had men of some knowledge
and wisdom on my counsel; I find I have none.
Was it polite, lords, to let this man,
this good man–few of you deserve to be called that–
this honest man, wait like a lousy footman
at the door of the room? Someone as great as you are?
Why, how shameful this was! Did my orders
tell you to behave so shamefully? I gave you
permission to try him as a counsellor,
not like a groom: there are some of you, I see,
who would hound him to death, more out of
malice and integrity, if you had the power;
which you shall never have whilst I'm alive.

Chancellor
Thus far,
My most dread sovereign, may it like your grace

To let my tongue excuse all. What was purposed
Concerning his imprisonment, was rather,
If there be faith in men, meant for his trial,
And fair purgation to the world, than malice,
I'm sure, in me.

In this matter,
my great Majesty, please allow
me to speak for everyone. The intention
of imprisoning him was to make sure,
if there are still good men, for him to have a fair trial,
and show his innocence to the world, it wasn't
done out of any malice, speaking for myself.

KING HENRY VIII
Well, well, my lords, respect him;
Take him, and use him well, he's worthy of it.
I will say thus much for him, if a prince
May be beholding to a subject, I
Am, for his love and service, so to him.
Make me no more ado, but all embrace him:
Be friends, for shame, my lords! My Lord of
Canterbury,
I have a suit which you must not deny me;
That is, a fair young maid that yet wants baptism,
You must be godfather, and answer for her.

Well, well, my lords, show him respect;
take him, and treat him well, he deserves it.
I will say this for him, if a Prince
can be in debt to a subject, I
am to him, for his love and service.
Let's have no more fuss, everyone embrace him:
be friends, for shame, my lords! My Lord of Canterbury,
I have some business which you must do for me;
that is, there is a sweet young girl who needs baptising;
you must be her godfather, and answer for her.

CRANMER
The greatest monarch now alive may glory
In such an honour: how may I deserve it
That am a poor and humble subject to you?

The greatest monarch now living would find this
a glorious honour: how can I deserve it
when I am just a poor humble subject of yours?

KING HENRY VIII
Come, come, my lord, you'ld spare your spoons: you
shall have two noble partners with you; the old
Duchess of Norfolk, and Lady Marquess Dorset: will
these please you?
Once more, my Lord of Winchester, I charge you,
Embrace and love this man.

Come, come, my Lord, do you want to avoid having to give a christening present?
You shall have two noble partners in the business; the old
Duchess of Norfolk, and Lady Marquess Dorset: will they suit you?
Once more, my Lord Winchester, I'll order you,
embrace and love this man.

GARDINER
With a true heart
And brother-love I do it.

I do it with a true heart
and brotherly love.

CRANMER
And let heaven
Witness, how dear I hold this confirmation.

And may Heaven witness
how much this action means to me.

KING HENRY VIII
Good man, those joyful tears show thy true heart:
The common voice, I see, is verified
Of thee, which says thus, 'Do my Lord of Canterbury
A shrewd turn, and he is your friend for ever.'
Come, lords, we trifle time away; I long
To have this young one made a Christian.
As I have made ye one, lords, one remain;
So I grow stronger, you more honour gain.

Good man, your joyful tears show your true heart:
I see the common opinion of you is true,
which says, 'Do my Lord of Canterbury
a good turn, and he will be your friend forever.'
Come, Lords, we are wasting time; I long
to have this baby made a Christian.
As I have unified you, lords, remain unified;

so as I grow stronger, you will gain more honour.

Exeunt

SCENE IV. The palace yard.

Noise and tumult within. Enter Porter and his Man
Porter

You'll leave your noise anon, ye rascals: do you
take the court for Paris-garden? ye rude slaves,
leave your gaping.

You'll stop your noise soon, you rascals: do you
think the court is a pleasure ground? You rude slaves,
stop your shouting.

Person within

Good master porter, I belong to the larder.

Good master porter, I work in the larder.

Porter
Belong to the gallows, and be hanged, ye rogue! is
this a place to roar in? Fetch me a dozen crab-tree
staves, and strong ones: these are but switches to
'em. I'll scratch your heads: you must be seeing
christenings? do you look for ale and cakes here,
you rude rascals?

Go and work on the gallows, and be hanged, you rogue! Is
this is a place for shouting? Fetch me a dozen crabtree
sticks, strong ones: these ones are just like twigs in
comparison. I'll scratch your heads: do you have to see
a christening? Are you hoping for free cakes and ale,
you rough scoundrels?

Man
Pray, sir, be patient: 'tis as much impossible--
Unless we sweep 'em from the door with cannons--
To scatter 'em, as 'tis to make 'em sleep
On May-day morning; which will never be:
We may as well push against Powle's, as stir em.

Please, Sir, calm yourself: it's just as impossible–

unless we clear them from the door with cannon–
to disperse them, as it is to get them to sleep
on the morning of May Day; that will never happen:
we might as well try and shift St Paul's as move them.

Porter
How got they in, and be hang'd?

How did they get in, dammit?

Man
Alas, I know not; how gets the tide in?
As much as one sound cudgel of four foot--
You see the poor remainder--could distribute,
I made no spare, sir.

Alas, I don't know; how does the tide come in?
I gave out as much punishment
as a good solid four foot club could distribute;
you can see there's not much of it left, sir.

Porter
You did nothing, sir.

You did nothing, sir.

Man
I am not Samson, nor Sir Guy, nor Colbrand,
To mow 'em down before me: but if I spared any
That had a head to hit, either young or old,
He or she, cuckold or cuckold-maker,
Let me ne'er hope to see a chine again
And that I would not for a cow, God save her!

I am not Samson, nor Sir Guy, nor Colbrand,
which would let me chop them all down: but if I spared anyone
who had a head to hit, either young or old,
male or female, cheat or cheater,
may I never have another woman
never again!

Within

Do you hear, master porter?

Are you listening, master porter?

Porter
I shall be with you presently, good master puppy.
Keep the door close, sirrah.

I'll be with you shortly, my little puppy.
Keep the door closed, sir.

Man
What would you have me do?

What do you want me to do?

Porter
What should you do, but knock 'em down by the
dozens? Is this Moorfields to muster in? or have
we some strange Indian with the great tool come to
court, the women so besiege us? Bless me, what a
fry of fornication is at door! On my Christian
conscience, this one christening will beget a
thousand; here will be father, godfather, and all together.

What should you do, but knock them down by the
dozen? Is this Moorfield for them to gather in its? Or have
we got some big strapping Indian brought to the
court, so that the women are desperate to get in? Good heavens,
what a great mess of spawn is at the door! I swear
by my faith, this christening will create a
thousand others; all the godfathers will become fathers, altogether.

Man
The spoons will be the bigger, sir. There is a
fellow somewhat near the door, he should be a
brazier by his face, for, o' my conscience, twenty
of the dog-days now reign in's nose; all that stand
about him are under the line, they need no other
penance: that fire-drake did I hit three times on
the head, and three times was his nose discharged
against me; he stands there, like a mortar-piece, to
blow us. There was a haberdasher's wife of small
wit near him, that railed upon me till her pinked
porringer fell off her head, for kindling such a
combustion in the state. I missed the meteor once,
and hit that woman; who cried out 'Clubs!' when I
might see from far some forty truncheoners draw to
her succor, which were the hope o' the Strand, where

she was quartered. They fell on; I made good my
place: at length they came to the broom-staff to
me; I defied 'em still: when suddenly a file of
boys behind 'em, loose shot, delivered such a shower
of pebbles, that I was fain to draw mine honour in,
and let 'em win the work: the devil was amongst
'em, I think, surely.

There will be more christening spoons, Sir: there is a fellow
rather close to the door, he's a brass smith by
the look of him,
for I swear that he looks as if he's been out burning in the sun;
all the ones who stand around him are
below him, they need no other punishment: that
firebrand I hit three times on the head, and three
times he blew his nose at me; he's standing there
like a mortar to blow us down. There was a
silly haberdasher's wife standing near him, who shrieked
at me until her pink cap fell off her head, which started such a commotion. I missed the fellow
once, and hit that woman, who cried out
'Clubs', and I saw far off some forty apprentices
draw their clubs to help her, they were all from
the Strand where she has her shop; they attacked,
I defended my place well; eventually they came to
close quarters, I still resisted them, when suddenly a
group of boys behind them, skirmishers, threw such a
shower of pebbles, that I had to withdraw
and let them capture the Castle; I think the devil was
helping them.

Porter
These are the youths that thunder at a playhouse,
and fight for bitten apples; that no audience, but
the tribulation of Tower-hill, or the limbs of
Limehouse, their dear brothers, are able to endure.
I have some of 'em in Limbo Patrum, and there they
are like to dance these three days; besides the
running banquet of two beadles that is to come.

These are the youths that roar at the Playhouse,
and fight for half eaten apples; nobody but
the crowds at the executions or the residents of
Limehouse, their dear brothers, can tolerate them.
I've put some of them in limbo, and they should stay there
for the next three days; and after that they'll get
a whipping from the beadles.

Enter Chamberlain

Chamberlain
Mercy o' me, what a multitude are here!
They grow still too; from all parts they are coming,
As if we kept a fair here! Where are these porters,
These lazy knaves? Ye have made a fine hand, fellows:
There's a trim rabble let in: are all these
Your faithful friends o' the suburbs? We shall have
Great store of room, no doubt, left for the ladies,
When they pass back from the christening.

Dear me, what a crowd there is!
They're still growing; they're coming from all quarters,
as if there was a fair here! Where are those porters,
those lazy scoundrels? You've made a great job of this, fellows:
you've let a great crowd in: are all these
your great friends from the suburbs? We shall have
plenty of room left, doubtless, for the ladies,
when they come back from the christening.

Porter
An't please
your honour,
We are but men; and what so many may do,
Not being torn a-pieces, we have done:
An army cannot rule 'em.

If you'll excuse us, your honour,
we are only men; and what our number could do,
without being torn to pieces, we have done:
an army can't rule them.

Chamberlain
As I live,
If the king blame me for't, I'll lay ye all
By the heels, and suddenly; and on your heads
Clap round fines for neglect: ye are lazy knaves;
And here ye lie baiting of bombards, when
Ye should do service. Hark! the trumpets sound;
They're come already from the christening:
Go, break among the press, and find a way out
To let the troop pass fairly; or I'll find
A Marshalsea shall hold ye play these two months.

I swear on my life,
if the King makes me pay for it, I'll have you all
in the stocks, at once; and I'll impose heavy fines
on you for neglect of duty: you lazy scoundrels;
you're sitting here teasing drunkards when
you should be driving them out. Listen! The trumpets sound;
they are already coming from the christening:
go, break through the crowd and find a way
to let the parade go through peacefully; otherwise
you will find yourselves in the Marshalsea prison
for the next two months.

Porter
Make way there for the princess.

Make way there for the Princess.

Man
You great fellow,
Stand close up, or I'll make your head ache.

You great fellow,
Move aside, or I'll make your head ache.

Porter
You i' the camlet, get up o' the rail;
I'll peck you o'er the pales else.

You in the posh coat, get up on the rail;
if you don't I'll chuck you over the fence.

Exeunt

SCENE V. The palace.

Enter trumpets, sounding; then two Aldermen, Lord Mayor, Garter, CRANMER, NORFOLK with his marshal's staff, SUFFOLK, two Noblemen bearing great standing-bowls for the christening-gifts; then four Noblemen bearing a canopy, under which the Duchess of Norfolk, godmother, bearing the child richly habited in a mantle, & c., train borne by a Lady; then follows the Marchioness Dorset, the other godmother, and Ladies. The troop pass once about the stage, and Garter speaks

Garter
Heaven, from thy endless goodness, send prosperous
life, long, and ever happy, to the high and mighty
princess of England, Elizabeth!

Heaven, with your endless goodness, give the
high and mighty Princess of England, Elizabeth,
a prosperous, long and always happy life!

Flourish. Enter KING HENRY VIII and Guard

CRANMER
[Kneeling] And to your royal grace, and the good queen,
My noble partners, and myself, thus pray:
All comfort, joy, in this most gracious lady,
Heaven ever laid up to make parents happy,
May hourly fall upon ye!

And for your royal grace, and the good Queen,
my noble partners and myself pray for you that
you will have all comfort and joy in the most gracious lady
Heaven ever sent to make parents happy,
may it come to you every hour!

KING HENRY VIII
Thank you, good lord archbishop:
What is her name?

Thank you, good Lord Archbishop:
what is her name?

CRANMER
Elizabeth.

Elizabeth.

KING HENRY VIII
Stand up, lord.

Stand up, Lord.

KING HENRY VIII kisses the child

With this kiss take my blessing: God protect thee!
Into whose hand I give thy life.

Take my blessing with this kiss: may God protect you!
I put his life in your hands.

CRANMER
Amen.

Amen.

KING HENRY VIII
My noble gossips, ye have been too prodigal:
I thank ye heartily; so shall this lady,
When she has so much English.

My noble godparents, you have been too generous:
I give you my hearty thanks; so shall this lady,
when she has learned to talk.

CRANMER
Let me speak, sir,
For heaven now bids me; and the words I utter
Let none think flattery, for they'll find 'em truth.
This royal infant--heaven still move about her!--
Though in her cradle, yet now promises
Upon this land a thousand thousand blessings,
Which time shall bring to ripeness: she shall be--
But few now living can behold that goodness--
A pattern to all princes living with her,
And all that shall succeed: Saba was never
More covetous of wisdom and fair virtue
Than this pure soul shall be: all princely graces,
That mould up such a mighty piece as this is,
With all the virtues that attend the good,
Shall still be doubled on her: truth shall nurse her,

Holy and heavenly thoughts still counsel her:
She shall be loved and fear'd: her own shall bless her;
Her foes shake like a field of beaten corn,
And hang their heads with sorrow: good grows with her:
In her days every man shall eat in safety,
Under his own vine, what he plants; and sing
The merry songs of peace to all his neighbours:
God shall be truly known; and those about her
From her shall read the perfect ways of honour,
And by those claim their greatness, not by blood.
Nor shall this peace sleep with her: but as when
The bird of wonder dies, the maiden phoenix,
Her ashes new create another heir,
As great in admiration as herself;
So shall she leave her blessedness to one,
When heaven shall call her from this cloud of darkness,
Who from the sacred ashes of her honour
Shall star-like rise, as great in fame as she was,
And so stand fix'd: peace, plenty, love, truth, terror,
That were the servants to this chosen infant,
Shall then be his, and like a vine grow to him:
Wherever the bright sun of heaven shall shine,
His honour and the greatness of his name
Shall be, and make new nations: he shall flourish,
And, like a mountain cedar, reach his branches
To all the plains about him: our children's children
Shall see this, and bless heaven.

Let me speak Sir,
for heaven orders me; and let nobody think
that the words I say flattery, for they will find them to be true.
This royal infant, may God always be near her,
although she's in her cradle, promises
to bring a million blessings upon this land
in the fullness of time: she shall be–
though few now living can see her goodness–
a model for all princes of her time,
and all who follow her: the Queen of Sheba
never had as much wisdom and beautiful virtues
as this pure soul shall have. All the princely graces
which go to make up a person like this,
with all the virtues good people have,
will be doubled in her. Truth shall be her nurse,
holy and heavenly thoughts her advisers;
she shall be loved and feared: her own people shall bless her;
her enemies will shake like a field of corn in a storm,

and hang their heads in sorrow: she shall bring good;
in her time every man will be safe to eat
what he has grown under his own trees, and to sing
the merry songs of peace to all his neighbours.
God will be properly worshipped, and those around her
shall see the perfect way to behave with honour, and derive their greatness from that, not from
their ancestry.
This peace shall not die with her; it shall be
like that wondrous bird, the maiden Phoenix,
another heir shall spring from her ashes
as much admired as herself,
so she shall pass on her greatness to someone–
when heaven calls her from this dark life–
who shall rise like a star from the
sacred ashes of her honour, as famous as she was,
that's how he shall be. Peace, plenty, love, truth, terror,
that all served this chosen child,
will then be his, and grow around him like a vine;
wherever the bright sun of heaven shall shine,
his honour and the greatness of his name will also
shine there, and establish new countries. He shall grow
like a mountain cedar, his branches will hang over the plains all around him: our grandchildren
shall see this, and thank heaven for it.

KING HENRY VIII
Thou speakest wonders.

You are speaking of amazing things.

CRANMER
She shall be, to the happiness of England,
An aged princess; many days shall see her,
And yet no day without a deed to crown it.
Would I had known no more! but she must die,
She must, the saints must have her; yet a virgin,
A most unspotted lily shall she pass
To the ground, and all the world shall mourn her.

She shall live to a great age, to the
joy of England; she shall have many days,
and there won't be one day without some good deed in it.
I wish I knew no more! But she must die,
she must, the saints want her with them; she'll die a virgin,
she'll go to her grave an unblemished flower,
and all the world shall mourn for her.

KING HENRY VIII
O lord archbishop,
Thou hast made me now a man! never, before
This happy child, did I get any thing:
This oracle of comfort has so pleased me,
That when I am in heaven I shall desire
To see what this child does, and praise my Maker.
I thank ye all. To you, my good lord mayor,
And your good brethren, I am much beholding;
I have received much honour by your presence,
And ye shall find me thankful. Lead the way, lords:
Ye must all see the queen, and she must thank ye,
She will be sick else. This day, no man think
Has business at his house; for all shall stay:
This little one shall make it holiday.

Oh Lord Archbishop,
you have ensured my prosperity! I never had
anything before I had this fortunate child:
these words of comfort have made me so happy,
that when I am in heaven I shall ask
to see what this child does, and praise my maker for it.
I thank you all. I'm most indebted to you
my good Lord Mayor, and your good brothers;
your presence is a great honour,
and you will find me grateful. Lead the way, lords:
you must all see the Queen, and she must thank you,
she will be upset otherwise. Let no man do
any work today; everyone should stay here:
this little child makes it a holiday.

Exeunt

EPILOGUE
'Tis ten to one this play can never please
All that are here: some come to take their ease,
And sleep an act or two; but those, we fear,
We have frighted with our trumpets; so, 'tis clear,
They'll say 'tis naught: others, to hear the city
Abused extremely, and to cry 'That's witty!'
Which we have not done neither: that, I fear,
All the expected good we're like to hear
For this play at this time, is only in
The merciful construction of good women;
For such a one we show'd 'em: if they smile,
And say 'twill do, I know, within a while

All the best men are ours; for 'tis ill hap,
If they hold when their ladies bid 'em clap.

It's ten to one this play will never please
everyone who's here: some have come for a rest,
and to sleep through an act or two; but I'm afraid
we have startled them with our trumpets; so obviously
they'll say it's rubbish: others came to hear the city
insulted, so they could shout, 'That's witty!'
and we haven't done that either: I'm afraid
that the only good opinion we're likely to hear
of this play at the moment will come from
the kind interpretation of good women;
for we showed them someone like them: if they smile,
and say it's good, I know that within a while
all the best men will be on our side; for it goes badly
for them if they hold back when their ladies tell them to clap.

THE END